OV

See More

Live More

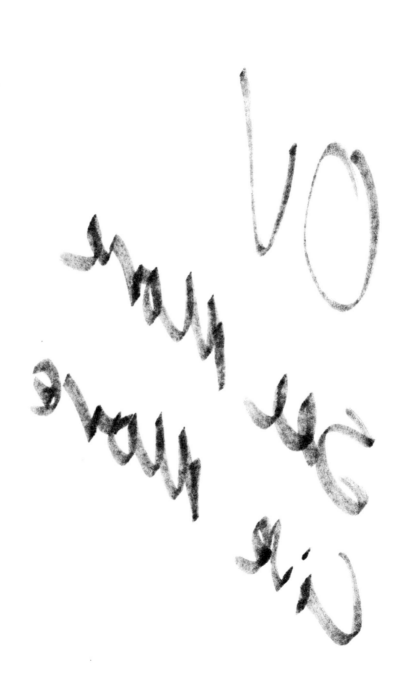

MY HELL & BACK

103 SURVIVAL TIPS

OPTIMUM VIZHAN

Order this book online at www.trafford.com
or email orders@trafford.com

Most Trafford titles are also available at major online book retailers.

Print information available on the last page.

ISBN: 978-1-6987-1674-9 (sc)
ISBN: 978-1-6987-1676-3 (hc)
ISBN: 978-1-6987-1675-6 (e)

Library of Congress Control Number: 2024906252

Trafford rev. 04/02/2024

 www.trafford.com

North America & international
toll-free: 844-688-6899 (USA & Canada)
fax: 812 355 4082

Contents

✢ Dedication ✢

This book is dedicated to
All the Service Men and Women
who did not and will not
get the chance to enjoy a life companion,
children, grandchildren and etc.;
for the rest of their lives,
due to their transitioning on while
serving their country.
And to those who have lost Love Ones,
Hoping to Share Your Lives with Them
for the Rest of Your lives;
Only to hear the News,
that Your Loved One
has Transitioned on
While Serving
Their Country...

*Here's a Sobering Moment of Silence
to Honor You...*

Now Unconditional Love's
Compassion and Strength Preserve
You Forever.

**And Bless You
and Your Loved Ones...**
forever and ever!

Author

✠ Dedication II ✠

This Book is Dedicated to My Wife
for Never Giving up on Us:
as a couple, as a family and as an
Inspiration to others;
to help them face their hells
head on.

I also want to thank...

My first son;
for Allowing Me to Live and Die
the Way I wanted to …
for Writing This Book for Me
About My life.

I Chose to Love You All by My Actions;
for they will and did speak louder than words
could ever speak.

Unconditional Love Bless My Family
and the families they have
forever and ever.

Richard

‡ Preface ‡

Son: Dad would joke from time to time about writing his memoirs someday. Those days did pass by too quickly. He and I have decided it's time to write his life story. Thinking too, it was a good past time hanging out with each other, while going through our Michigan Winter. Then come out of our man caves, with a published book about his life story. Awesome, let's do it.

Dad: I was in Two Wars; One with Korea and one with My Wife.

Son: In both, dad had to learn to come at peace with himself and Unconditional Love. This would allow him to focus on facing his hells head on, and witnessing Unconditional Love walking him through them at the same time. Establishing him again with new resources, that would take him through the next season of his life.

Son: Dad's life started at the end of the Great Depression in the 20th Century, on his father's large self-sustaining farm. His dad's large farm supported the needs of his family, those who lived in the local communities and those who drove a few hours for his hard cider and meats.

Son: His father's home was a big farm house, built for a big family; two stories, two stairs one each end of the house going to the upstairs, gas lights, full walk-in pantry, big wood burning pot belly fire furnace between the living room and dining room, big wood burning stove for cooking for the family and hired hands, cellar, front and east side full wrap around porches. Lots of windows, his sisters had one big window in their room. His mom and dad had a big bedroom down stairs with its own stair way to the upstairs. No inside plumbing. The water well pump was inside and in the kitchen; for convivence to make up for the outhouse toilet. My dad would laugh every time he said, in the winter when it was freezing, he would lift the second story bedroom window open and pee out it. His parents would find out about it; when they saw the yellow ice cycles hanging from the porch roof.

Son: Two barns; one large barn that held the large livestock: cows, horses, etc. and the smaller barn held the smaller livestock: chickens, goats, sheep, rams, etc.

Son: Dad believes his dad or grandpa planted an Apple Orchard when he/they was/were younger, from which he sold apples, hard and sweet ciders. His mom grew gardens that provided vegetables for the family and the local communities. While his siblings took turns milking the cows for milk, cream, cottage cheese and his favorite - ice cream.

Son: A creek ran through the farm and a small pond just east of the farm house, up by the road.

Son: Dad had five siblings before he was born; one sister and four brothers; all a few years apart from each other.

Son: Gypsies with covered wagons full of goods to sell would go by the farm, on regular bases. If they or others didn't have a place to sleep at night, his dad would let them sleep in the barn with the animals.

Son: Looking back, I can see the season's dad's life went through. From the day he was born to the day the family buck sheep rammed him into the steel wheel on the tractor. That's where he got his big "V" shaped scare on his forehead. From the buck sheep ramming him into the steel wheel to the day he met his lifelong sweet heart. From the day he met his sweet heart to his flower shop. From the day he started his flower shop to being drafted into the Korean War. From the day he was drafted into the Korean War to his marriage. From the day he was married to returning from the Korean War. From the day he returned from the Korean War to the farm house. From the day he moved into the farm house to his sisters-in-law's home. From the day he moved into his sister-n-laws to his flint home. From the day he moved into his flint home to his wife's transitioning. From the day his wife transitioning on, to the publishing of his life story. From the day he's life story was officially published to moving out of his last home he built. From moving out of his last home he built to moving in with me. From moving in with me to transitioning on himself. They would all start with Unconditional Love setting him up and then end it with someone trying to set him back.

Son: The purpose in writing dad's memoirs is to inspire people not to give up on their lives, when they find themselves facing their own hell; to relax, wait upon Unconditional Love to show them a way out. Be it near dad's death experiences; on the farm, in war, driving vehicles, building homes, marriage, heart attack, a bypass and loss of his loved one.

Dad: Ok. Enough of the commercials, let's get started.

Son: This preface is the same preface in dad's book *Hell & Back*, by Optimum Vizhan. Sold on Amazon.

Son: All of his life story is documented in his book, *Hell & Back*, by Optimum Vizhan. That book goes into all the details that took place; during those near-death experiences, throughout all of those events in his life. Along with a brief listing of these Hell & Back 103 Survival Tips.

Son: Dad intentionally wanted to go into deeper details on all these Survival Tips. But our life changing events together, prevented us from having the time to expound on these Hell & Back 103 Survival Tips.

Son: If you did and or when you get the chance to read his autobiography; about his life in Hell & Back, then you'll see how I was able to go in greater details with these my dad's … *My Hell & Back 103 Survival Tips.*

AND NOW AS MY DAD WOULD SAY...

Ok.

Enough of the commercials,
let's get started 😊

✠ My Hell & Back 103 Survival Tips ✠

S on: One of the rewarding opportunities in helping dad write his life story in book form; was asking him what nuggets of wisdom/thoughts he had, that got him through and as well obtained from; while going through his Hell and Back experiences. It was like Unconditional Love giving me a second chance in life, to connect with my father as a son. After a few Local Diner strawberry short cakes, Dad came up with a 103 Hell and Back Survival Tips. For us to consider, when going through the different hellish seasons of our lives.

Son: In this My Hell & Back 103 Survival Tips we are going to put those original 1 to 103 tips into five categories versus dad randomly saying them and me writing them down.

Son: This way we can put those categories in the Table of Contents. So that you can zero in on the ones that your looking for in a particular area of your life right now.

Son: The categories are Spirit, Mind, Body, Skills, Life, Relationships and Family. Seven categories. And we will start in that order as well.

Son: The Spirit is the core of who we are. The Mind connects the Spirit and Body. The Body allows us to have physical emotions. The Skills give us more options to work with. The Life is what our Spirit, Mind and Body navigates through. The

Relationships are sharing the same life experiences together. The Family is allowing other spirit mind and bodies to share in these Life experiences as well.

Son: Ok. That might of got a tad deep there.

Son: Why am I still starting out each paragraph with Son? It's out of respect for my dad. These are all my dad's tips and me just observing him from a son's life perspective. Growing up with him, interacting with him.

Son: And fascinated enough to wanting to understand how he thinks, makes his decisions and how he survived all those near-death hellish moments. What was his mindset going through them all?

Son: Once we went through his life and had all his deep memories and experiences written down in a manuscript. I was able to see clearer how he increased his odds in making it through all his hellish near-death experiences...

Son: I said dad, are you at total peace with your life? He said, yes.

Son: Him being at total peace with himself and wanting to connect with all of life, put his mind and body into the right position to increase his odds in surviving all his hellish near-death experiences.

Son: Ok. Enough of the commercials. ☺

✝ Spirit Survival Tips ✝
QTY 10

Note: I kept the same numbering sequence in my dad's autobiography book Hell & Back, but categorized them in this book. Make sense?

1. Have No Thoughts of Dying. Understand living. I think God figures it out pretty even. He gives us a chance to live a full life. Some people like to rush it; by getting sick, drive to fast. My dad was 96 when he pasted.

Son: His dad at 96 was a healthy man in and up to his transitioning on. He NEVER went to the doctors. A few of dad's siblings decided to take their dad to the hospital to get "checked" out, a few years before his transitioning on. His dad was so pissed off; that he was throwing his bed pan at the nurses, every time they were coming through the door of his room. Remind you this guy grew up in the late 1800's. A long lineage of long life spans.

Son: My dad was the same way. Which makes sense why they lived longer lives. They never thought about dying. They focused on getting through it and to the other side of whatever they were dealing with.

Son: So why did they transition on then? Good question. From my personal experience with them as they were transitioning on, they were at peace with their lives and they had no other reason to live in this world. In the case of my dad, his free movie sweet heart had transition on four years before he did. She was all of his life. He made a lot of bad decisions in his life but he was always around her; she was his heart beat. Each day he lived without her, his will to live was decreasing. To the point he just let go and peacefully transitioned on, like he was finally back with her in her arms, once again.

Son: It was in making what seemed to be good decisions; were in reality were bad decisions without knowing it, at the time of doing them. From those bad decisions, he acquired these 103 Survival Tips. These tips would increase his survival rate the next time.

6. God's the Boss. Man can't do what the hell He wants. God gets man to do His work; but if doesn't, He can.

Son: Whatever is going to happen is going to happen. Humans can't stop it. They can be a part of it, if want or not. It's going to happen anyways.

Son: General Example: Like if you live in an area on the planet, that has four different seasons. Winter is coming and it randomly snows, when it's in the mood. Lol. I can get a snow shovel to deal with the snow or not. If I refuse to get a shovel, snow blower and or pay someone to move it. Then I will no doubt cause more work for myself, by getting stuck in it off an on. Or be forced to stay home for the day. YEA!! Lol. Either way, it's going to snow.

Son: Personal Example: Say me and my spouse doesn't want any children at this time in our lives. We DO EVERYTHING we can, **to make sure we don't** have any children. And then BOOM. My spouse tells me one day, hey honey I'm pregnant. No Joke. Seriously. We're going to have a baby nine to ten months from now. I'm speechless, while my mouth is wide open in disbelief. A few months go by, and yup, her tummy is sticking out there a lot more. Next day, we're at the store buying maternity clothes.

13. Always Have Time to Stop and Smell the Roses. It's just a saying. You get out of it whatever you want out of it. Don't really have to stop, just keep on a smelling.

Son: My dad had a natural nak at weaving wit and humor together like he was a Master Tibetan Monk at it. I only witnessed a few times where someone could outwit and humor him. Momentarily. Then he would out do them as well. Everyone would drop to their knees laughing and or standing at awe. Priceless.

Son: Even though dad, loved being busy making and doing things with his hands all day. He would take like five-to-fifteen-minute breaks; just at the right moments to enjoy that special moment with a person and or scenery in creation. Like a rose.

Son: Keep in mind; my dad had these near-death hellish moments in his life, that made him more aware to appreciate the small things and life more. Not to take life for granite. Be sensitive to the beauty of creation around us and or at least smell the beauty – if you don't have time to enjoy it.

19. Raise Hell. – So, Hell Knows You are in Charge. Get a little excitement. Change your normal routine. The surroundings you're in helps get you through your teenage years. A lot of company. There's a place for everything. A time.

Son: In another words kick hell in the Rearend so hard that Hell will want you to leave. Do an extreme make over first, so that you leave your mark and they'll remember, who was there long after you leave. (*Note: this add on is in dad's original book Hell and Back.*)

Son: Dad started at the age of five to embrace challenges head on. LITERALLY. The family Pet Sheep/Ram was like how we have our favorite dog pet today. Dad at five years old. FIVE. Was walking towards the ram, like he was going to head butt the ram. The ram was playful in nature and lowered it's horns down, as dad got closer. Once in contact, the ram would lift his head and horns fast. This would end up tossing dad into the air. Dad was now airborne and laughing. This was normal and a fun summer day thing, to do on their farm...

Son: ...One day though, they both got really into it and came at each other harder than normal. My dad became a missile in flight now. Heading straight for the old school tractor's steel wheels. Dad's head hit the V shape welds on the steel wheels for traction. His was knocked out cold on the ground with blood all over his face and head. His dad was in shock. Ran over to his prize well loved ram, thinking his son was dead. Raised the 200+ pound ram up in the air with one hand and cut off the ram's head with a butcher knife in the other hand. It was a sobering moment for all. The ram was their best pet ever and his son appeared to be dead by the tractor steel wheel.

Son: Dad came too eventually. This was in the mid to late 1930's; before hospitals and emergency centers were in driving distance, for most communities. When dad opened his eyes, his best friend ram was dead. His dad's broken heart was at least starting to heal, seeing his son was alive.

Son: My dad was in tears, that his best friend ram was no longer alive to play with. But thankful, he was alive. His head healed up with the V shaped scare on it. Every time he looked in the mirror, he could see that V shaped scar on his head. Especially as he got older and his hair line, started to recede.

Son: From that day forth, at FIVE years old, no matter what my dad faced, he faced it head on. Knowing no matter what the loss was going to be, he was going to be scared by it.

Son: The family's favored best pet ram, knew what the outcome would be playing with my dad like that. Dad's dad was a butcher. And butchered, seasonally the cattle, pigs and sheep they had on the farm. But knew out of love for my dad, he had to do this for his best friend… to prepare him for all those near-death experiences, he was going to have in his life…

Son: Stopped typing. I'm crying right now. Thinking about all that love; that family's favorite best pet ram had for my dad. To the point; he sacrificed his life to prepare my dad for all those near-death experiences, he was about to have later in his life.

Son: Priceless friendship to have.

Son: Going to stop here for now. Writing down that memory, from all those times dad would tell me about that story, finally hit home. To what dad was really saying.

51. Never too Old to be a Kid. I think a kid has the knowledge and ambition to do what they do. We all have to go through that kid stage.

Son: Dad was an active kid. Milking cows at 6am and again at 6pm. Then every once in a while, the neighbor kid would come over watch and talk with him. To liven the conversations up, my dad would squirt the kid in the face with the milk from the cow, he was milking. Nice shot. Dad would take off running because the kid was so mad at him, for squirting cow milk in his face. The boy was a lot heavier than dad, so dad would always out run him. Dad knew the right routine on how to shut a conversation down.

Son: Dad walked to school M-F, no school buses back in the day. From what I remember he said, he walked 1 and ½ miles to school. One way, then back again. As they walk by the neighbor's house, the kids from that house would come out, and walk with them. Quite a small crowd of kids would be walking to school together. Dad mentioned the older kids would have the little kids ride on their shoulders, while they were walking to school. A lot of looking out for each other.

Son: Dad dropped out of school at 16. Raised gladiolas on the banks of the creek that ran through the family farm. Then, sold them at the Farmers Market.

Son: Dad said, he was all naturally wanting to do these things as a kid. The natural talent is already in the person, it will naturally come out. The kid stage brings it all out them.

56. If I had to do it all Over Again I would do it. Cuz you could add in or out, if want to do; to complete it.

Son: Dad defiantly had no regrets from ALL the experiences he dad. Zero. Even through all the near-death hellish events he was at peace. He was relaxed to the point; if there was going to be any negative consequences, then his body would have the higher odds in surviving it.

Son: Like with the family best pet ram. He would do it all over again. He got the rush in being airborne at the age of five. And he thought it was cool to have the V scare on his forehead. He referred to the V on his forehead for meaning "Victory." The thing he would tweak, if he could relive that, would be somehow save the family's best pet ram from being put to death.

86. Each Season has Its Own Time. Summer, Fall, Winter and Spring; we go through four seasons. Breaks up your year; variety. We do a little bit different in each one. If we had one season, we wouldn't like it. We would view life from that one season.

Son: They go through cycles that are generally subtle and gently move in and out of. Once in a while they'll make a surprise entrance or exit, but mainly gentle. The shorter to longer daylight times helps get creation ready physiologically for the next change. And vis-a-verse. It starts out exciting, we enjoy it then it gets to be the "new norm." The next season starts up and we get excited again.

Son: The seasons force us to change our routines. New routines are refreshing, then they become dull again. The secret is to change our routines before they become dulling again. Like change the living room view before it becomes just the "same" living room. All it takes is switching two chairs, or moving the couch on a different wall. Bam. Everyone in the family is "Refreshed Again. If interested in mastering routine changing before life gets boring, read my book. *"Can My Life Change"* by me Optimum Vizhan. On Amazon.

Son: The different seasons of routines, give us a more variety of views to appreciate life in a deeper way.

88. We're the Greatest Miracle that God Created. – ref Og Mindo.

Son: Dad was personalizing a book he read and I originally botched up on how the author spells his name.

Son: The book dad read was *The Greatest Miracle in the World*, by Og Mandino.

Son: It made an impression on him so much, that he made it apart of his mind/heart set; to surviving his near death/hellish moments of his life.

Son: The idea of a Creator creating humans, the way we are, gave dad a surreal peace in believing everything will be ok. A relaxed state of mind. They say, the people who have the highest rate of survival in a motor vehicle accident, are the ones who are the most relaxed. Be relaxed, one has to be at peace with their circumstances. Even if they don't like it, but are making due and looking for an exit plan.

Son: Dad was relaxed in his head on the truck-to-truck accident in his early thirties. He said the oncoming truck went in his lane, so he went in the other lane. The head on truck went back to his original lane, then went back to dad's lane... As Dad swerving back into his lane. BAMM! The oncoming truck, hit dad head on. Both trucks were totaled. Both were alive but knocked out cold. The front window shattered into tiny pieces and laying on dad, like it was a powdered glass blanket. The steering wheel smashed into dad's chest on impact and broke his ribs on both sides.

Son: We were up north at dad's cabin. About 100 miles away. Mom tells us, dad was in a bad accident and we need to leave asap.

Son: A couple of days later dad was home, getting rest and healing up. Family and Friends would be coming over regularly to see how dad was doing. The times I was in the room with dad and these people, dad was acting like it was nothing. He would tell jokes about it and say he, needed a break anyways. Oops. Pardon the pun. That wasn't punny. Lol.

Son: Dad had once again, survived a very frustrating hellish moment and lived to talk about it, with total peace.

90. Take Time to Enjoy the Season We are in – It Seems to Even Itself Out. No Season was fast.

Son: Once again. Like we shared in the last one **#86**; dad having those near-death experiences, he would appreciate even more, the seasons of his life. Regardless if it's painful, fun, sobering, etc. He noticed they go full circle. They innocently start out as a new cycle/phase in life. Then one starts realizing things are generating new patterns and routines. We get use to and or least in managing them. Then things start to subtly change again.

Son: Much like the seasons. Dad grew up on the planet, where there are four distinct seasons. Each season has its routine. Spring starts out warm and nature is blooming back into life, we get use to it. Start mowing lawns full of new growing grass. We get use to that, then the summer heat kicks in. Adjust the clothes we're wearing. And now we're moving lawns full of weeds, because the grass stops growing, due to very little rain.

Son: Just when we got use to that, Fall kicks in. The weeds stop growing and now we're mowing lawns, full of dead leaves. Just about when we get all of the dead leaves that fall from the trees mowed, we're winterizing the mower. Picking up a snow shovel and shoveling snow off our driveways.

Son: With dad living in this type of seasonal patterns, he learned to enjoy each season. In the spring season, he would be tending the new plants and trees that were growing, open up his cabin. In the summer, he was boating, skiing, playing water volley ball and camp fires. In the fall, he would close up his cabin for the year, harvest gardens, pick apples, trim trees and play cards with his family on the weekends. In the winter, building snow mans, sledding, remodeling his home and or building the next one; we would be moving into.

Son: Then with him naturally enjoying them already, he would then apply this to his life. The seasons his life was going through. Starting from scratch a Flower Shop business at 16. Yup at 16. Sold it and with the money bought wedding rings to marry his wife at 20. The day after his honeymoon, he's shipped off to the Korean War. Comes home to have a family, works and builds homes after his day job. Builds a cabin out of telephone poles. Yup. Back in the day they were made out of solid cedar wood. Buys a farm and works it. Subdivides it. Sells it and consolidates for retirement. Gets a place for out of state winters, where its warmer.

Son: Then lace that all together with his near-death hellish accidents. This guy accepted all that; to become a master at enjoying every season of his life, he was in.

Son: And all of that above was just the framework of his life. A ton of stuff was happening on top of all that, that was super intense at times.

102. It's Very Important to Keep God in Mind All the Time Because That's Where it All Starts and Ends.

Son: Life is deeper than just being born, going through the phases of being a human. We might be fortunate enough to experience a relationship with a spouse and have a family. Maybe even have a good friend as well.

Son: When we get to the part in our lives in asking the question, who created us and why? If we think it's all by chance, then we have the excuse to do whatever we want. That increases the odds in having near death experiences more often. That's where my dad was. He was fortunate enough to survive and decide there must be a Creator who created him.

Son: If it's the Unconditional Love Spirit, then there must be a greater purpose. The purpose would be to have eternal friends versus being all by oneself. It starts with the Creator wanting to have eternal friends. And ends with the Creator having eternal friends.

✠ Mind Survival Tips ✠
QTY 13

2. RRRRRRRRRRRRRR. Get Focused. Look Out. Rrrrrrrrrrrrrrrr.

Son: Dad your funny, witty and full of wisdom all at the same time. Of which it helped you through all those multiple near-death hellish moments, you experience and live to tell about. Then you summed all that wisdom up, in the one repeated letter "R." RRRRRRRRRRRRR. *Amazing.* Who could imagine that hearing the RRRRRRRR would mean, I'm getting focused... Look Out! Lol.

10. Play Hard, Work Hard and Sleep Hard. Good to play hard. When we were kids, we played hard. Keeps the old blood circulating to get into low spots. Gives you good rest. Keeps your body up and kicking. If haven't learned by sixteen just horsing around then.

Son: I just realized dad's last comment on, "if haven't learned by sixteen just horsing around then." Forgot all about it.

Son: If a child hasn't mastered the playing hard, working hard and sleeping hard routine by sixteen. Then odds are high they will never know what's the deeper meaning; of why we should work hard, play hard and sleep hard. Our adult life is a mirror reflection of child life. If we haven't had the drive too when we were a child then the odds are high, we won't have the drive too when we're adults. I personally believe that.

Son: The combination of working and playing hard during the day, will set the spirit, mind and body up for wanting to sleep hard at night.

Son: How do we tie this back into being a hell and back survival tip? The tip is in mastering sleeping hard. When my body gets a really good sleep time then my body will be able to react quicker to close calls, tough decisions and the got to keep moving mindset. If I don't get a good night's rest then most of us all know, it's a slow day the next day. Even if I can live on a few hours of sleep, that will only last for a few days.

Son: Regardless, we all LOVE a good rested up night's sleep. Even when we are children as well.

Son: Working and playing hard, also means the mind/heart set of knowing what you're doing and wanting to accomplish within that day. Versus a have no goals mind /heart set. It doesn't matter. So, what. Etc.

11. Laugh a Lot. Makes yah smart. Gives yah something to think about.

Son: You have to be smart to be funny. As in a colorful, imagination and witty thought process. And the ability to pull it altogether within seconds, to make people laugh.

Son: Handling frustrating and embarrassing situations with a laugh. It's tough to do. Believe me. I would rather move on, but my mother had mastered a tad of this. But dad was the Tibetan Monk of Laughing A lot.

Son: Mine started at the 3rd grade. My dad was into butch to the skin haircuts. Us new generation coming uppers; wanted our hair longer, down to your shoulders – longer. He ignored my haircut preference. Took me to the barbers. Butch hair in less than five minutes. I looked in the mirror and all my hair completely gone, with some nubs left. Lol.

Son: Next day was school and I was wearing a hat, to cover up my head of hair nubs. We were all standing by the door, waiting for our teacher to let us in. The kids were teasing me about wearing a hat. The teacher shows up, to let us in our class room.

Son: Everyone takes off their coats and head to their seats. I was the last one standing, refusing to take my hat off. The teacher told me to take off my hat. I didn't. She said one more time, in the tone you better take your hat off or else tone. I slowly proceeded to take off my hat. It was now off. The WHOLE CLASS BUSTED OUT LAUGHING at ME! I was looking at teacher to get them to stop laughing at me. She didn't. I was in silent pissed off mood for the rest of the day.

Son: I went home to tell my mother ALL ABOUT IT. She didn't say a word. Waited to when I was all done. Then she said, Did You Laugh Back? I said No. I went onto explain my reasons why the teacher should stop them from laughing at me.

Son: Day Two. It was a repeater. Everyone busted out laughing again and the teacher didn't do NOTHING about it. I was now in Day Two Pissed Off.

Son: Got home and told mom, the same thing with reasons of justifying being pissed off. She said, Did You Laugh? I said no. End of discussion.

Son: Day three. Same routine but everybody got more ballsey, while waiting for the teacher to open the door for us. Hmm. Ok. Time to nip this in the rearend. Since the teacher has made it clear she's not saying a thing while enjoying the show.

Son: I thought, ok. We'll milk this one to the bone. I did everything exactly the same as I did, for the last two days. Even taking off my hat r e a l s l o w. Without smiling. Same facial expressions. It's like I got best actors award.

Son: The class BUSTED OUT LAUGHING Again. I was amazed that me just taking off my hat; could make them laugh that hard, three days in a roll. Blows my mind. I looked at the teacher the same way I did for the last two days. She was dedicated at letting all those kids make fun of me. Cold hearted, I was thinking...

Son: So, I BUSTED OUT LAUGHING SO HARD that it was louder then all their laughing. They all INSTANTLY stopped laughing. YUP. Then I looked at the teacher and her jaw dropped, with her mouth wide open speechless. Took my hat off with a smile and walked to my seat. With all confidence in owning the class. It was Priceless.

Son: So, I couldn't wait to get home to tell my story to my mom. BUT, I thought, what they hay. I will do the same with my mother, just to see if she can give me the same advice all three days.

Son: Same word for word conversation to my mother about my bad day at school. She was all ears like the last two days. Never interrupted me. Waited until I was all done talking. Then she asked the dedicated advice, Did You Laugh Back? I was amazed at her dedication for all three days, in saying the same thing as well. Now I know why. She knew the power at laughing at people; versus being upset, angry, etc.

Son: This time I said, YES. She said, how did they take it? I said, they all instantly stopped laughing and the teacher was speechless. It was priceless mom.

Son: From that day on, I started laughing at people who were making fun of me. And was amazed on how it shuts up mockers consistently. So, we had a lot of fun with it.

Son: Dad and Mom, must have had to mastered this to earlier in their lives, for them to be able to give me this advice. Thank you, dad and mom. Priceless.

Son: Oh, what's even more ironic? They've long transitioned on and I'm getting my haircut a few weeks ago. I started to noticed the barber was ignoring my request on how I want my haircut. They kept cutting shorter and shorter. Maybe they'll stop here and clean it up. Nope. So, I started telling my story about my butch haircut when I was in third grade. Still cutting. Everyone in the barber shop is listening to my story; like they were right there with me in third grade. I was milking the story. The barber was in it so much, they kept cutting my hair. All with scissors, like they were using an electric shaver. So I'm looking in the mirror and seeing the same haircut, I got when I was in third grade.... Everyone was intently listening, at this point. So I told them the PUNCH Line. I BUSTED OUT LAUGHING AT THE WHOLE CLASS. They laughed and so did my barber.

Son: Then my barber knowing they too went to far in cutting my hair and cautiously said, how do you like your haircut? I said, PERFECT. It's looks exactly like you love and enjoy cutting hair. The barber gently smiled but knew what I was implying. Yup. I've grown up a tad and learned several ways on how to LAUGH BACK, without Laughing Hard Out Loud.

16. When Making decisions and others think your nuts take it like a man and do it anyways. It will just work out. They don't know what they're talking about.

Son: I'm really really thankful to see this from being my dad's son. You see it first hand, behind the scenes and hearing the people's responses are priceless. Versus experiencing it as a third party, trying to reason all the different "opinions to draw a conclusion.

Son: Like my dad making a cabin out of old cedar telephone poles. Yup. You read right, telephone poles. They thought he was "nuts". Lol. He worked for an utility company, in the early 1960's. They were upgrading their telephone poles from cedar to pre-treated much bigger poles. He asked them, can have the cedar telephone poles. They said yes. He got a whole boat full. Now they really thought he's going to the "nut" house.

Son: His brother had a saw mill. I'm three years old and remember this like it was yesterday. I standing off to the side, cold, but wanted to be apart of it. Watching a saw mill, mill the telephone poles into different sizes to build a cabin. They're still thinking dad's nuts. Dad's all in and focusing on utilizing his time versus explaining all the details to them. You know, actions speak louder than words.

Son: Dad sees me shivering pretty bad. He stops the cutting and takes me home. I'm not happy but the warmth persuades me to go home. He goes back and finishes the job. There was so much wood cut out of the telephone poles; it took him several trips, to take it all to the new cabin site.

Son: Fast forward to the day, he's laid it out all on the ground. And now all his hecklers, are there helping him out putting the pieces together. He was building an A Frame cabin. It was so cool to see everyone on the ropes, pulling the A's up in the air and securing them to the subfloor. Priceless. All the people that were calling him nuts are now ALL IN as well.

Son: One more from a pile of many, your "nuts" man. He was looking at an eighty-acre farm. He paid $48,000 for it and those same people that called him nuts on building a cabin, are calling him nuts with this one too.

Son: Oh, I was at that cabin a few days ago and those cedar poles are just as strong as they were in the 1960's. They got to be at least 70 years old. Impressive.

Son: All those hecklers have transitioned on and that cabin still stands today. Not one of those cedar beams are rotten. Not one.

Son: Back to dad's your nuts for buying an eighty-acre farm for $48,000 story. It had a beautiful twenty-acre woods in the back of the property. Next minute, I helping mom and dad name the roads to the new subdivision dad was designing for the farm. He was getting all kinds of heckling. He ignored it all. The subdivision plan fell though and his hecklers were saying, see we told you so.

Son: He acted like he didn't hear a word they were saying. He took the old barn down and used the wood to remodel the farm house. I was helping dad every minute I had. It was a blast too me. I even made some tree camps out the wood from the farm house he was gutting to remodel it. He ended up subdividing the farm into larger chunks. The county was pissed at first but legally couldn't stop him, due to how the zoning laws were set up. Dad was smart. He knew how to use their words and rules against them.

Son: What's even funnier is, the utility company that he was working for, wanted to buy 17 acres from him. Yup. At higher than market price for it. AND, they gave him the rights to farm it. So, get this. He doesn't own it now, doesn't have to pay the land taxes on it, but he gets the harvest crops from it.

Son: Fast forward, he's done a ton of other things with the farm. Me too. I got to raise animals on it and with my money I earned from selling the straw bales, have a micro pond dug next to the horse stalls. Yup, dad let me raise two horses on his farm. Priceless… 10 years later, felt like 30 years from all the things we did together as father and son, all the hecklers were no where to be found. He turned that $48,000 farm investment into a few hundred thousand dollars.

Son: Really didn't have much to show for it; but had a ton of fun with it, growing up with him in the 1960's and 1970's.

Son: Priceless dad. So, dad is saying, regardless of what people say, if you're the only one who believes in your endeavors then that's all that matters. *Do them all the more.*

20. Slow Down and Think What You're Doing. Not enough in one thing to keep you busy all the time. Slow down. Grow older. Pace paces. Slow paces. Grows and goes through stages it seems to go good. Balances out.

Son: Pace yourself, think about it from all angles versus rushing to get it done. Enjoy the process. The faster we go, the less it means to us. The quality of the process is more enriching.

30. I'm going to Stick in there, so that I can say I stuck it out.

Son: Stick and Stuck. Saying it like that, makes it stick out more. The tacker the Stick the stronger the Stuck will be. Lol. I just realized this; when thinking about this in a deeper way. Lol 2.0.

Son: How sticky the stick is will determine how stucky the stuck is. That goes for anything in life; relationships, quality of craftsmanship and one's life itself. Here's to being super sticky so we can have a super stucky life.

Son: Was my tack tacky enough; to make my thoughts on being sticky, stick out more? Lol.

33. We can be Stupid at Any Age. Don't have to know everything.

Son: It's a good starting point, to be in the mindset of wanting to learn, something new at any age.

Son: We should be in the mindset of wanting to always grow in our lives. Like when we were infants after being born from our mother's womb. Always curious to understand, to learn how to roll over for the first time. To learning how to take our first steps, to fully walking without assistance. That process kept us young at heart.

Son: It's interesting and sobering at the same time; to look over the years and notice the correlation to people aging. The less people want to learn and grow, the slower their lives become. The slower their lives become, the more their lives shut down.

Son: My dad was mentally wanting to grow in his life and was healthy all of his life. A couple of speed bumps tried to slow him down, but mentally he kept growing in them. He had quicker recoveries from the norm and bam, back at it again.

Son: It was about a few months up until he transitioned on, that he didn't have the drive to want to grow in his life anymore. He did miss his wife like no other. The more he stopped wanting to grow, the more his body was shutting down. To the point, he had to start wearing an adult diaper. Three days later after dealing with wearing an adult diaper, he passed on. Sobering.

53. Focus 100% on the job you're working on. Once you understand the job 100% then you'll have time to think of the next job or going forward easier.

Son: My dad was a Master Tibetan Monk with this too. He wasn't disrespectful to people and animals that would come around him, while he was all in on a project. He stayed focus. In a matter of a couple of minutes people would be helping him and or moving on.

Son: This allowed dad to get the projects he was working on done much quicker. His attention span on a specific task was extremely high. Whereas today, I'm hearing the average attention span is 3 to 5 seconds. Makes a lot of sense why people are taking years to accomplish something, versus days, weeks or a few months.

Son: Then his key reason tip why. Master the task 100%. Then while doing that task automatically, we're free to think about the next project. And or, completing it quicker to enjoy one's life more. Without having all these unfinished jobs, littering our lives where ever we go.

54. Never take anything serious. Something doesn't go normal or planned; think it over to keep it going. Sometimes you put stuff in that doesn't do a thing for what you're trying to do. Sometimes you can back off and let it work out.

Son: Did I mention that my dad was a Master Tibetan Monk at this? He honestly didn't take anything serious to put himself in the mindset of being able to quickly adjust to any situation. It increased his odds of getting through a task and or problem much quicker. Versus getting mentally all jacked up about it. Which in the long run, is just a BIG waste of time. So why not nip it in the rearend upfront and be open for other ways to accomplish your task at hand.

Son: This is how my dad could work hard, play hard and sleep hard. He would work his day job, come home build or remodel a home and take time to play with us, before diving into between the bed sheets. Lol. Seriously. All naturally without being stressed out.

Son: Note: He mastered this so naturally, that we were moving into a new home about every 2 to 3 years.

Son: Oh, and go to the cabin on the weekends during the prime summer months. Priceless.

69. Have Good Humor.. It's good to have humor. Don't want to be serious all the time.

Son: Humor was dad's way of holding everything together. It was like he was crocheting humor in, with and to hold all the moments we had together as a family. Then when you step back and look at it, it looks like a beautiful afghan blanket. *Aaawe....*

Son: For the record, dad never crocheted. That was mom's with her closed eyes, art. She would crochet while watching tv, having conversations and sometimes I swore, while she was sleeping. Lol.

72. Slow is Better than Being Fast. You can think better when you're slow.

Son: Dad understood that rushing to do something, really meant, that the person really doesn't want to do it. It's like their being forced to do it. He knew that would increase the odds of not being done the best way. And going back to refix it, because it was slapped together.

Son: The quality of the craftsmanship and relationships are at a higher quality.

Son: If someone is rushing through on a job all the time then more than likely; *they'll be the same way with their relationships.* Then regularly going back to fix the damage – if they're in the mood and or forced to.

76. If I Wake Up in the Morning and Don't Have a Tag on My Toe Then I know it's Going to be a Good Day.

Son: ☺.

Son: He made a quick assessment of his life; after waking up from sleeping hard, by looking at his toe. No tag, no time to complain. Good to go. Day light is burning and the cows got to be milked.

Son: He would mention from time to time; he doesn't have time to let the grass grow, between his toes.

Son: This also kept him in the sober reality; that he needs to utilize his time, while he can move around. That way if he can't, then he'll have time to heal up and or take a vacation from doing projects.

89. Give Everything to God because He's going to give you everything. He's already done it. If we don't take it, we lose it. If we take it and do right with it, it will be good to us. We should be smart enough to know. If not, they know something about it; even if it's a little bit. Grow up, go to school, buy things; God's furnishes all that, plus.

Son: Dad recognized that all the details of all creation freely flow together. From the smallest component to the grandest, they all flow freely without the assistance of humans. That takes an Unconditional Love Creator to do all that. So, in accepting that, recognize it and flow freely in it. Trusting if the Creator did all that, then the Creator will take care of all the rest, for us as well.

Son: If we don't then will never see it and experience it.

Son: Even in the little bit people have, should realize in having a choice to do whatever they want to. Be it to help creation or destroy it. An Unconditional Love Creator loving them so much, that the option of choice is given to them.

Son: So, in a deeper meaning of what he is saying is. We have the option to give or keep. If we give, we will have everything. If we keep, we will have nothing.

Son: When we give life, we are freely flowing with life. If we keep life then we are not flowing freely with life.

‡ Body Survival Tips ‡
QTY 5

8. Stay Away from Booze. Always had around house. Dad had hard cider around from the apple cider mill. We would have several barrels of cider and hard cider. Dad would always let several; seven to nine, drunks hang around. Dad would give it away. Dad would not charge them. They would hang out half the night. Mom would have one of my brothers get hard cider up from cellar, drag up steps and roll up steps. Throw out, drain out of barrels onto ground. Good sign to drunks that all done. They went back to the bars. They would get so drunk they would piss their pants; because you can get hooked on it.

Son: Note: This is my dad talking about his dad. His dad was a generous successful big farm man. He had his on-site apple, apple cider and hard cider store. His cattle, sheep, milk and cream from the cows and crops as well. Plus, he was a butcher. So, his dad pretty well had all the bases covered to earning income from all types of sources. My dad would say his dad set up his farm; so that he could be making money every month of the year, from it.

Son: Oops. I had to come back and plug this in. His dad would take the products he produced to the Farmers Market regularly as well.

Son: Now mentioning all this, now I know where my dad got his work ethics from. Watching his dad do all those projects throughout, all the months of the year. Each season, he had something else to do for income.

Son: His dad could handle being drunk as well, but the drunks couldn't.

Son: I hear some people have the bacteria in the stomach to break down certain alcohols, to the point they are not affected by consuming it large quantities. I can vouch for that. One of my children can consume large amounts of alcohol; and can talk and make decisions like they didn't drink anything at all. On several, different occasions over several years. It's impressive.

Son: After dad's mom decided to end the daily free drunk parties; by busting all the hard cider kegs open, his dad and his love to get drunk buddies would go to the closest bars.

Son: This was one of dad's favorite stories to tell about his dad. After a hard day's work, his dad would go to one of the local bars. His dad's dad was smart enough to homestead a farm by three local cities. One in the north, one in the south and one in east.

Son: His dad would alternate between bars. He would start out at one end of the bar front counter, bartering what he had with someone who had something he needed. And or take orders for any of his farm products he was selling. One by one. When got done then he proceeded to get wasted on his favorite alcohol beverage.

Son: Once he got tanked, he would ag someone on to fight with him. Sometimes he would have to get them pissed off, so they would fight with him. And surprisingly every time, they couldn't take him down. Then another guy would jump on the pile, on trying to take him down. Another. Another. Another. Yup and another, for a total of six guys riding him, like he was a human merry go around. Lol. He was as strong as an ox.

Son: His dad got most of his muscle back in the day; when the ox would be pulling the one blade plow, and he would have to man handle the direction of the plow. Over a 150+ acres of farm land. Impressive.

Son: So, all in all; his dad made use of the end of the daily drunk parties by going to the local bars, to barter and sell his products. Then interact with them with a good old fashion bar room brail; to prove whose the strongest of the bunch, for cheap entertainment. You imagine going to the bar today to sell something, get drunk and then start wrestling each other on the floor. Lol.

Son: My dad was keen enough to know, if they can't handle their booze, then don't waste your time with them. Plus, was they really friends? Nope. They only came to his dad's farm, because he was giving it to them for free. When his mother busted the hard cider barrels to pieces, they all stopped coming over. And went to the local bars.

Son: His dad was a very generous man. He had a lot of land and he utilized it; to be earning something monthly from it, every year. He became wealthy from it. Word got out and the quality of his hard cider; that people would drive in their buggies, to get it. Yup. Horse and buggy days folks. From just over a hundred miles out.

9. Eat a Lot of Ice Cream. One of my brothers and I would make ice-cream, when the rest of the family went to town. Easy to make. Eight quarts of ice-cream. Jersey cow eighty percent cream. We had that one cow just for ice-cream. Just a desert.

Son: I can vouch for that. Especially growing up on the farm my dad bought, the one everyone called him "nuts" on. He had a wooden bucket with a cranking device on it. The device would hold a metal cylinder container that would hold the ice cream making ingredients. Like milk, etc that would turn into ice cream as you would crank, to spin the container around in circle. Inside the container was paddles that would mix the ingredients even more. The container was like four inches smaller than the wooden bucket, so that you could pack ice between the bucket inside wall and next to the metal container itself. The cold and the friction, made the ingredients turn into ice cream on the spot.

Son: Steady cranking would get you ice cream in about thirty to forty minutes. Then let it set for a tad. Pull the metal container out of the bucket. Take the metal lid off and pull very slowly the paddles out. This is where you can sneak in some licking the ice cream, off the paddles. And have a good reason to, "I need to test to see if the ice cream tastes Gooooood." Lol.

Son: Scoop out and put in a bowl and good to go.

Son: My dad loved ice cream so bad, he made it with his brother, when the rest of his brothers and sisters went to town with his parents. Yup. A big family of seven children; five boys and two girls. So that they could have more ice cream to themselves.

Son: A good sign of an ice cream addiction. 😊

Son: But it makes sense. Back in the late 1930's early 1940's there wasn't as much desserts, sweets and snacks as we have today. It was probably more-healthier anyways. All natural ingredients, straight off the farm.

Son: Plus. Having the best type of cow milk to make the best tasting ice cream.

Son: Speaking of cows. My dad would have to get up earlier enough to milk the cows by six am. Yup. He would go into details, about making sure all the tits were milked. After double checking, then you would have to "stripped" the tit. This is done by using the thumb and the index fingers. Gently pinch the tit area by the utter, then slowly go down the entire length of the tit. The idea is to get every drop from every tit on the utter. Why this extreme? The cow will stop producing milk. As long as the tits are being milked this way; the cow will keep producing milk, as it would for the cow's baby calf. It's neat to know that functions naturally. The calf will stop drinking their momma's milk, when they've grown old enough to live without it. I know, interesting farm tips.

Son: Reflection Moment Time: It's amazing how much more we learn from living and growing up on a farm versus anywhere else.

Son: Oh. Ice Cream making the old fashion way was the main staple in all of our birthdays, in my family. Plus during mile stone birthdates with the greater family, on my mom's side. She had three sisters. Yup. And no brothers. Image growing up with three other sisters and no brothers.

Son: Oh 2.0. My dad's dad, when he got up in age and was starting to "check-out", his brothers and sisters were taking turns watching their dad, for a week at a time. So that means my dad would be watching him every seventh week. That's what makes bigger families why much cooler. More siblings to help out when needed. Ok... So, my dad would make old fashion ice cream, for his dad. His dad would be smiling from ear to ear.

Son: As time went on into 1990's, even though the old fashion making ice cream went to the wayside, dad still loved his ice cream. Ice cream sandwiches, going to ice cream parlors and or just sitting down and eating it straight from the carton. That was dad's best part of the day. Any day.

31. Get Good Rest so We can Have a Good Day. Get all drained out if don't.

Son: This is dad's key to being a non-stop train in accomplishing all those projects on time, with high quality and not feeling rushed in the process days.

Son: Working hard and playing hard produces a good rest. Taking a more laid-back approach to everything produces a, I'm having a hard time trying to sleep. And when I do get to fall asleep, it's a restless sleep. I end up spending a lot more money on things, that will help me sleep better. And all I had to do was work hard and play hard.

Son: It's crazy to see, I would rather be laid back and pay for a monthly gym membership to get my "work out". Versus work and play hard on the things in my life. AND it doesn't cost a penny. Hmmm.

Son: Again. These are personal observances of my dad, while growing up with him in his home(s).

40. Learn How to Play Hard. Gets all the benefits of moving the body.

Son: Hmm. Here's another tip, but said in a different way. My dad realized; his key to accomplishing a ton of good things for his family and himself, was to be in this heart/mindset, period. Period. And just to make the point, Period.

Son: It does take persistence in building muscles up, in baby steps. To the point one day, you find yourself really getting into what your playing. This is the learning part.

Son: Another example is, dad would get us all out of the cabin of "watching tv" versus engaged physically playing; by setting up the badminton net. And say, who wants to play me badminton? Dad was so good; us kids would be on one side and he would be on the other side by himself. Lol.

Son: He was like a secret pro-master at badminton.

Son: We were trying our hardest, he would do a backwards body shot, without even looking at us. We would be laughing so hard,` that we missed our return shot back to him.

Son: Sometimes, dad would wear silly hats to distract us. He would hit the birdy so hard; it would get stuck up in the trees, on our side of the badminton course. That means we would not only have to knock it free from the tree, BUT also hit it back to his side, if we wanted to get the potential point.

Son: My dad was a master at playing hard and teaching us, how to play hard ourselves as kids.

Son: He did this as well in playing horse shoes, boating, skiing, inner tubing – before it was commercialized, playing cards, building sand castles, arm wrestling, playing dice, snow ball fights, snow sledding, water volley ball and even going for car rides in the wooded areas.

Son: Priceless all the memories of playing with my dad. It's not only good for one's body. It's defiantly required for making enriching family moments.

98. Sports Keeps Your Body Healthy.

Son: This is the funniest one. Notice how he didn't add anything after saying, "Sports Keeps Your Body Healthy." Hmmm. Maybe because he never played on a sports team. Never. AND he never was into watching sports on tv.

Son: Hmmm 2.0. Why is he including this one, as one of his survival tips?

Son: From my personal experiences of observing all the things my dad did, as his son. The first thing that comes to mind is, maybe he knew some families don't learn how to play hard, so by at least joining a sports team, they'll learn how to condition themselves mentally and physically. Plus get a ton of practicing in when "competing" against other teams, within that sport. This would give them the full circle experience of learning how to get into playing hard.

Son: This would be the second option. The preferred option is with your family. So that the family can have MORE deeper enriching moments together. This helps complete the whole family experience. These embedded experiences, increases the odds for the child to have a good-enriching experiences with their children someday, in the future.

‡ Skills Survival Tips ‡
QTY 17

1 **2. Everyone Should Know How to Milk a Cow.** To see where the milk comes from. Some kids like to learn; some don't. Secret to milking a cow; be gentle. Don't pinch them or they'll swatch you with their tail on back of head. Every morning, they will be filled up with milk. Twice as big as my hand. We had twenty-four cows. Milk a cow in fifteen minutes. Milk all tits. Use both hands. Gently squeeze until done. Then do stripping. Two fingers thumb and index; get another two cups. If didn't strip them they would dry up. All of us, milking cows before school and before supper. Feed them too. Like to eat hay and grain. Carried water to them. Modern farms had water faucets. A bowl held about gallon water. We milked cows, feed, then let go out to pasture graze around. Planted clover. One hard summer; dry up hay, still eat it. Seems to even out. No problem. Feeding hay, clover and alfalfa. Stalls in, hook them in brace. Stations for each cow to hold them.

Son: Dad said, he started milking cows at five years old. With his work ethics, wouldn't be surprised.

Son: Learning compassion and gentleness early in life, sets the tone for the rest of one's life.

Son: Him being the last son of his family, would slowly put pressure on him. As his older brother's left home and got married, dad was left to milk more cows to pick up the slack.

Son: What's cool though, when gold backed the dollar, prices stayed pretty much the same. So, all the brothers would buy up tangent farm properties next to their dad's farm. They still lived together, helping each other farm their lands. But had no time to milk the cows.

Son: Twenty-four cows divided by five boys equals about five cows per boy. One brother leaves home, it's six cows per boy. Another leaves, it's eight per boy, Another leaves, it's twelve cows per boy. Dad said it took about fifteen minutes, that equals about three hours in the morning and three hours in the evening. Sobering.

Son: The older dad and his brothers got, the more they noticed this. Some of them, would not take the time to gently strip the tits. Some of the cows would slowly stop producing milk. His dad could see it and wouldn't say much about it. Knowing the family was getting smaller and less mouths to feed.

Son: Back in those days, people were starting to see the cities getting bigger, due to the factories popping up everywhere." The pre-do-it-for-you packaging was a convenience of being able to do other things in ones life.

Son: Never the less; that experience of knowing how to and miking the-cows morning and evening routinely every day, made up dad's core in doing everything else in his life. How he interacted in relationships, work life, building homes, playing and even facing his hells head on.

Son: It's amazing to see what we do in our childhood; is basically how we are going to be handling our adult lives in general. That's deep. If we're honest with ourselves and see what we did during our childhoods.

Son: Now being unbiased. Put up a mirror to it and we will see the reflection of the same reactions, in our adult lives.

Son: With this being-honest-to-ourselves knowledge, we can increase our children's lives to be more enriching as well as their children lives. We need to foster these types of experiences.

Son: I know these options get fewer and fewer due to our circumstances. But the secret is in utilizing what we have in front of us. However how small it is, work and play hard with it. This will be worth more than all the other "bigger and better" things out there.

14. Every Kid Should Grow Up on a Farm. Every kid doesn't need to grow up on farm. Go where he wants to go. Do everything on the farm. Sets you up to go where ever you want to go. A lot of different jobs on a farm.

Son: And this summarizes what we said lastly in the last tip, before this one.

25. Play A Lot. It's more fun. Stop once and awhile and get your work done.

Son: Lol. It's funny that he says this, because he was working on projects more than he was playing. It was the other way around. He would stop every once an awhile to play. But he would make the point to play every day.

Son: It's the emphasis on when playing, be all in it. Not just go through the motions because someone else wants to play. It's I want to play and I'm all in heart/mind set. This creates the synergy within the other people playing with you, to want to play with you more often. Since they are always having fun with you, they are always looking forward to playing with you again.

26. Be More Careful. Listen to learn yourself to know when to be careful.

Son: This is a tough one. We're always justifying this is all we have to do, to get this done. Then something happens. It ends up taking longer and or we are stopped dead in our tracks.

Son: Versus getting all jacked up about it, relax, do some deep breathing. Then learn how to listen to ourselves subconsciously, telling us to be more careful.

Son: If I easily get jacked up all the time, then nothing is ever going to change in my life. Being honest with myself.

Son: I'm better off in the long run; to learn how to listen to my subconscious telling me how to do something better, in baby steps.

Son: Remember how we as babies could see everyone walking around us, but we couldn't. We weren't in a rush. *We didn't even know what being in a rush meant.* Lol. We would start by learning how to roll over. Then sitting up. Then standing up by holding onto something. Then when we felt confident, we took our first step. Was we jacked up every time and all the time, throughout that process… Nope.

Son: Well, maybe one or two of us was. If so, then odds are high, they were ALL jacked up while going through the delivery process. Lol... The space in here is getting too tight... The delivery tunnel was too tight... Being in the open air was too cold... Where is my umbilical cord? What do you mean, I got to start doing things for myself?... Why is it soo bright?... On and on and on...

Son: Versus. Ok. This is what it feels like to be in tight spaces. Relax. It must mean we are about to be born, into a new season of our physical life experience.

Son: Hmm this delivery tunnel is tight as well. Now it makes sense while the last few days while being in my mother's belly was tight. It was to get me conditioned up for this.

Son: OH Dang. Being outside my mother's belly is way too cold. What are all those burr feelings on my skin? Hmm.. So, we'll be experiencing different temperatures in this physical world.

Son: Why do I feel like I'm hungry? Where's my umbilical cord? My life line between me and mom is gone. Who took my life line to my mommy? Hmm... I must have to do things in this physical world by myself, to take care of myself. Mom!!! But it comes out as NEH NEH! NEH!! NEH!!!

Son: What is all the bright light? I can't see. Hmm... How can we turn off that bright light? Must be different types of light. One for sleeping and one for being awake? MOM!!! NEH!!!

Son: Learning how to listen to ourselves in baby steps, will help us to avoid some hellish moments in our lives.

28. We Don't Know What We're Saying until We can Say it Backwards.

Son: *Priceless.* No matter how many times I heard my dad say this, I go back to being five/six years old.

Son: While trying to learn my ABCs for public school, I would say dad, I know my ABC's. Then I would start saying them. A B C D E.... X Y and Z! I was so proud of myself. Then my dad's delayed soft tone words came from his mouth, Can You Say Them Backwards? I looked confused and say no. Then he would say, you don't know your ABCs, while smiling.

Son: I was really confused then. My public-school teacher was saying one thing and my dad was saying another.

Son: It was brilliant on my dad's part. On sparking within me, my own uniqueness of who I am. This is true love of the parent for the child, in helping the child to harness who they are as a person... in this physical world. Versus relying completely on the education system to tell me what to think and how to think and why I think this way. Go deeper; research and connect with my inner self, in a deeper way. No one loves me more than myself, except for Unconditional Love Creator.

Son: Once my dad's words absorbed into my heart, I lite up like a huge candle. Being able to say my ABCs backwards. So, this was on my heart and mind 24/7. Seriously. I would be falling asleep to Z Y X W V U T... C B A. Lol.

Son: At first, I kept it to myself. Then as I got more confident in saying my ABCs backwards, I would start talking to the kids that were around me. I would tell them the story of my dad saying; you don't know your ABCs, until you can say them backwards. All their reactions were the same. Confused. A few would laugh. Then I would start saying my

ABCs backwards to them. Their looks on their faces, was like the minds were going crossed eyed. Lol. *I loved it.*

Son: When practicing with the kids around me at school was done, then I went to my dad. This was like a few weeks later. I said, Dad I know my ABCs! He looked at me like go ahead and start saying them. I said A B C D... X Y Z! He said it again with the same compassionate tone. *Can you say them backwards?* I didn't change any of my facial expressions at all. And said, Z Y X W V U T... C B A!

Son: My dad lite up and said, *Now, you know your ABCs son. That's good son.*

Son: It was a priceless moment; in understanding the wisdom my dad had, in teaching me about having the experience of thoroughly understanding the skill your learning. ANY SKILL, just by learning your ABCs backwards. Brilliant.

Son: This is really deep. If I don't learn my ABCs backwards then anything I pursue will always be: 1, 2, 3...10. Where as if I learned my ABCs backwards then I could do: 10, 9, 8 ... 1 and get a better-results because I thoroughly understand what I'm doing. Front wards and Backwards. Brilliant 2.0.

37. Keep One Tire in Plow Furrow and Your Eyes on a Fence Post a Half Mile Out and You'll Plow a Straight Line.

Son: What does looking at Fence Post have to do in Plowing a straight-line bro? Lol.

Son: Everything when you're on the tractor and your plowing the fields. You're on a time line. Especially if your trying to dodge the rain storms.

Son: Me being new to this, I was caught up in watching the plow flip the dirt over. Sometimes a stone caused the plow to flip up. Stop, go back and redo. If can't, then dig the stone out. Dad was avid about having me go around the farm after it was plowed, to pick up all the stones. We would put them on a wood sled made out of poles. Then drive it up by the farmhouse and stacked them up next to the house. They looked real pretty, after the rain washed them off.

Son: So, my eyes were on the action. Where the plow was digging in the ground and what was in the dirt when it was being flipped over.

Son: Dad said after he gave me his lesson on plowing, your turn. He took my place; I took his place on the driver's seat. He didn't say a word. I should have known from learning my ABCs, how this was going to work out. ☺

Son: It was priceless. Not a word came from my dad's mouth. I get at the end of the sixty-acres and start to turn around, to do another plowed patch. I was so proud of myself until I looked back at my job. ☹

Son: I look at my dad with some shame on my face, but trying to back pedal. You know, just like when I was learning my ABCs. He let me finish. He let the silence speak for itself. That was another deep lesson he taught me, on how we can speak a whole lot more with our silence then we can with our words.

Son: Then he broke the silence with, look at that fence post. In my mind, it sunk in, look at the letter Z first then everything will fall into place.

Son: Dad took back over the driver seat to do the next path to straighten the rows all back up. When done. He stopped the tractor, got out of the driver's seat and looked at me. I knew he was giving me another chance at it.

Son: This time I took my eyes off the plowing flipping the dirt over, to looking at the fence post about a half-mile out. It was tough at first. Believe me you. I wanted to look at the ground so bad. I would slightly try one eye on the plow and one eye on the fence post, but that was messing with me. So, ok. This is me learning to ignore the plow.

Son: I gotz to the end of the path and was turning the tractor around, to get in position to plow another path back. ☺

Son: Dang. Dad was right again. If you want to do and end the job right; focus on your end results. The target versus throwing the dart. Or in this case, the work versus the plow and effort. I know. Priceless and Brilliant at the same time.

Son: Wait, there's a tad more. So, when I got the tractor and plow ready to plow another path back. I couldn't see a fence post to look at. *Dad! There's no fence post to look at? What do I do?* Dad said, it doesn't have to be a fence post. It can be a certain tree and or any other object. Pick the object that will allow you to plow a straight line any time. **WOE DUDE**. Another epiphany going off in my head, like beautiful fireworks show.

38. The Best Time to Milk a Cow is between 4am and 6am and then again between 4pm and 6pm. If you don't milk them at the same time they'll dry up. If not regular time, they'll stop giving milk. Have to be consistent. Can't change a cow's milking time. If don't line up with it, she won't give any milk.

Son: Wow. I forgot about this one. It's not only the gentle stripping of the cow's tits, it's the timing. It has to be twice a day and it has to be the same time on the clock. 4 am to 6am and 4 pm to 6 pm. It's amazing the biological clock that cows and creatures have. And the sensitivity to it.

Son: They don't get all jacked up about it, if you do or don't milk them. If you do then they'll keep producing, because for obvious reasons you must need the milk. This is the innocent love of a cow, when they are milked the old fashion way versus through an assembly line. Of which I have seen horror stories that have brought me to tears. It was so sobering, that the abuse they go through, I've stopped drinking cow's milk.

Son: And if you don't milk the cow, then the innocent love of the cow, will stop producing milk for obvious reasons, you don't want the milk. It's as simple as that.

But yet mind blowing how simple it is.

Son: We are either all in or we're not. Oh, some may say, I wanted to but this or that happened; so that's why I couldn't do it. There all excuses.

Son: I've been guilty of this several different times. But when I'm honest with myself, I really wasn't all in. It sounded good, so I went through the motions. BUT my motions were not all in. So why should I expect to get any milk from the "cow" I'm pursuing?

Son: *Is this what you call* MOO WISDOM? Lol.

43. Do it until it Becomes Automatically Naturally. Do what you want to do. Changing times of milking a cow, the cow will dry up sooner than later.

Son: No matter what you pursue as a skill and or just daily chores around the house, learn it until you don't think about, what your doing. This allows the mind to be more aware of its surroundings, so nothing ever surprises you. Takes you off guard.

Son: *And back to the cows. Just because I know how to do something automatically naturally,* **sometimes it doesn't mean,** *I can do it when ever I want.*

44. Have Fun Working Hard. It lets us enjoy it better. Time goes by faster.

Son: This is another extra plus in learning something automatically naturally. This allows us to have some fun at what we are doing. The time will go much faster because we won't be looking at the clock all the time. Plus, it will increase our output without feeling exhausted.

Son: Plus 2.0. This is apart of our work hard, play hard and sleep hard mind/heart set. Wouldn't be surprised, if all those additives we need to take: to keep us going; to keep us in a good mood and keep us sleeping, will not be needed anymore.

47. Do it until it Becomes Automatically Naturally so that You can Enjoy it.

Son: Oot Oh. Didn't we just cover this? This is the end results of doing what you love to do. What is that one thing you love to do; that no matter how long you do it, you don't get tired of it. It actually energizes you, like your not even tired. Yup. Mine is writing. I could write for four hours, after a big day, tired and ready to go to bed. But within a few minutes, its like I drank an energy drink – without drinking it.

Son: If your struggling with this then take the time to see what your heart's passion is. What do you do easily, that helps other people out?

Son: Harnessing your passion will be worth more than you can imagine. You'll love your life more and people will love being around you more.

52. Hold Your Stick Up Straight. It's possible.

Son: *Whaaaat?* It builds stamina, focus and better reaction times; due to the persistence of holding it up and steady. The longer you hold it up; the longer the stamina, longer the focus and better the reaction times.

Son: Still sounds crazy? Start out with a small wooden stick. Then move up to a larger wooden stick. Then move onto a small metal pipe. Then a larger metal pipe. Feel the difference, as your going to heavier objects in baby steps.

58. Don't Go too Far into Something Until you Learn it.

Son: This goes along with, "the-watch the fence post" while your plowing the land tip. Dad taught me to focus on the end results versus getting all fixated on the details at hand. Now remember we can do this; if we have learned, how to do it automatically naturally.

Son: Take in baby steps. Don't rush it. Enjoy the process.

Son: And there's a big difference in wanting to ride a horse versus knowing how to ride one. Start out slow, get use to understanding the new routines.

59. We will always have to Learn How to Milk a Cow and Plant a Field.

Son: Regardless if I do or don't get the chance to grow up on a farm to learn these skills, I'm going to be drinking and eating food.

Son: However, these two skills are the fundamental components of having more enriching experiences with: myself, my spouse, my family and loved ones.

Son: As reference earlier with learning how to milk cow: we learned it was the gentle touch of the thumb and index finger, to strip the tits on a cow. If we don't use this technique this way then the cow will dry up. This technique mimics the way the mother cow's calf milks their mother.

Son: This teaches us, it's the gentle touches with have our loved ones and with all of creation, that gives us the deeper enriching relationships. If one is harsh, quick and ignores, the cow dries up. Our relationships dry up. *I know that was deep.*

Son: Planting a flied isn't as easy as it sounds. You have to plow, disc, drag, plant and pack the field. Plowing might turn up some rocks.

Son: If you don't do it in that order, the harvest won't be as much. It's important to take the rocks out and put them in a pile somewhere. *Rocks grow when they are under the surface of the soil.* Yup. They are crystals. Plus, they will damage the other pieces of farming equipment.

Son: This teaches us, it's the preparation and the maintenance of the land, that gives us a good crop of food. So, in turn if we want life time of healthy enjoyable relationships, we need to prepare and maintain our relationships on a regularly basis. And at times; they might be obstacles that will affect our relationships, in a harmful way. Stop and remove the rock/obstacle from our relationship. Put it off to the side, so that it can stop growing and making more problems later on. *I know that was so much more-deeper.*

Son: Dad was that way. He didn't talk much; but it's like he was thinking about those types of correlations, in everything he did. And just automatically applying those correlations thereafter in his life.

Son: Dad spoke more with his actions then he did with his words. He used that wisdom, in how he interacted with people. If the person's words didn't match up with their actions, then he just made a quick light conversation with them. If the person was speaking with their actions, then he had a deeper conversation with them.

Son: Or, simpler. If he could see the actions then odds are high, they are speaking the truth. If he couldn't see any actions then the odds are high, they don't know what they are talking about. Another words... *A lot of Non-Sense.*

61. It Pays to be a Good Cook for Oneself, Family and or to Sell.

Son: This one is a tad funny. Dad didn't cook much, but he did sure LOVE his wife's cooking. Oh man, mom would knock everything she cooked out of the park. Her canning food was amazing as well.

Son: But those day's when mom wasn't around, to do something more important. Dad was the family chief. No matter what he slapped together, it was good as well. He didn't go to get details of making it. *It was like a dump, cook and go meal.* Lol.

Son: So again, this is him observing someone, in this case it's his wife.

Son: She knew her herbs and spices like she knew how to crochet an afghan. When she got done, it not only tasted good it looked good. No matter the size of the crowd, it all tasted good.

Son: And that's the selling part. She didn't make money at it, but she worked for non-profits to feed the people having hard times and or different types of mile stone celebrations.

Son: We had no problem doing the dishes afterwards. Mom! That was **DELIOCIOUS!!!**

62. If Your too Short Stand on a Piece of Paper.

Son: 😊 wait... 🙂 .... Every time mom would try to reach up for something, dad would ask her if she needed a piece of paper to stand on? She was a short woman. Built solid. She could swing a mean bowling ball down the alley, swat me on the back side of my head with her eyes closed and slam a door real hard when she was pissed off at dad.

Son: But her weakness was her height. She was like four foot nine inches tall.

Son: Every time dad would make that comment, she would just ignore dad. Dad would laugh.

Son: Every once in awhile when I see someone having a hard time reaching something, I ask them if they want a piece of paper to stand on. They laugh. Most people now a days, haven't heard of that funny witty saying.

87. Pack Light. Don't have to worry about everything.

Son: This goes with becoming very skillful at life's survival necessities. I can pack lighter items because I can improvise, if necessary, along the way.

93. The Top Three Investments: Invest into Something Easy, An Easy Hobby and Playing Sharper Pool.

Son: Dad was a master at all three of these. He knew the importance of balancing them out, to reduce his risk of making a bad investment.

Son: Dad would invest in a railroad stock. Why? Because every major industry uses the railroad at some point or another. If one industry isn't doing good then the others will keep the trains moving.

Son: The easy hobby dad chose was remodeling. Most the time it was just a hammer, screw driver, saw and a tape measure. He could do about any small project with the inexpensive tools.

Son: Now the Sharp Pool Player investment. That's why you pick a basically risk-free investment and an easy hobby. So that you have time to play some pool for cheap entertainment. And oh man, dad loved his pool playing. He was so good at it; he could play with his eyes shut. Ball goes in the hole, he smiles.

Son: Note: He looked at the hole the ball was going to versus looking at the pool stick hitting the ball. Like the same with plowing a field – look at the fence post way out versus the plow.

Son: This would bring the family together real fast, when dad would pick up his pool stick.

Son: If we both won a game of pool then we had to play a tie breaker game.

Son: Everything kind a shot was legal as long as you hit the Q Ball first. Combos, jump balls and miss Qs all counted. The more people were around that wanted to play pool, dad would choose the game, so that everyone could play. Versus waiting for the game to be over.

Son: Example: If they was an odd number of players then we played nine-ball. Hit the number one ball first, then two, etc. The nine-ball had to be the last one to put in the hole. You could make a combo shot to get the nine-ball in sooner, to win the game faster. Like hit the two-ball first, to make it hit the nine-ball into the hole. Those kinds of shots, got the crowd roaring and wanting to play another game.

Son: Dad loved playing sharp pool, just to see the people's facial expressions. Priceless. He could hit the Q ball sharp and boom, you heard the hard sound of the ball going into the hole. And you're thinking, *Dang*. He's good.

Son: My mom. 😊 She gave dad a run for his money. It's like they play pool in their sleep, they played it so well. They loved playing pool so much; they bought a pool table, for the farmhouse. Turned the one car garage into a pool room.

Son: This is one game she could play without standing on a piece of paper. Lol.

Son: Every time you watched them play pool, it was like they were on a date together.

Son: Mom and dad called themselves Professional Slop Pool Players. They did all kinds of crazy shots that were so cool, they would call them good versus playing by professional pool player rules.

Son: Everyone once in awhile mom would surprise with putting two balls in at the same time. She hits the Q ball and bam. Two other balls go in. Our eyes would go so wide; the first time we seen her do it, I gave her the pool player nick name, *Two Ball Sally.*

Son: Ok. Enough of the commercials. I was going to put a smiley face here, but thought. *Hmm.* Let's not wear that out.

Son: Why sharp pool as an investment? It's fun and most everyone likes to play it. But the most important part is... you have to learn how to focus; think about how much you need to swing the stick and to coordinate it, to hit another ball into the hole.

Son: Plus; when you're in tight spots, you have to learn how to do bank shots off the inside cushions of the pool table, to hit the right ball.

Son: All those "basic" skills help with everything else in my life. I need to focus; I need to time coordinating things together and know how to get out of tight spots in my life.

Son: It blows my mind; how dad had the knack of taking the simple things, we do in life and making them into metaphors for living better lives. Plus; perhaps increasing our odds in surviving the hell and back events, that might occur in our lives.

‡ Life Survival Tips ‡
QTY 22

3. **Stay Out of Trouble. Be Smart.** I use to get into a lot of trouble. My trouble making friend lived a few miles down the road from my dad's farm. Wrestle a lot. No boxing, wrestle.

Son: This is an understatement. *Seriously*. There's a dark side to dad. Which will be a whole book in itself. *Title will be* **Hell and Back *the dark side*.** By me, *Optimum Vizhan*.

Son: He was a brilliant, sincerely caring, resourceful and an awesome dad. Plus, his wit and humor were priceless. He is... what the over abuse cliché says, the life of the party. If you met him and did things with him, you would never know.

Son: I would have never known. *Seriously*. BUT I came home one day after school and my mom wanted to talk to me about something. She couldn't take it anymore. She needs to talk to someone or she's going to go crazy. So, after every afternoon after school day, my mom would talk to me for one to two hours a day. The rule was we must stop talking about it before dad gets home.

Son: I was shocked, devastated by all the details my mom would tell me. I was fourteen years old, in the early 1970's. Society was defiantly nowhere near as it was open now.

Divorce was not allowed. You had to suck it up buttercup. Which compound the problem.

Son: My mind is scarred for the rest of my life, until now writing this. My parents have both passed on, so I can openly write about it respectively, but in a better perspective.

Son: It's amazing, he was dedicated to being an amazing father. He would come through that door and looking at him, I swore they are two separate people.

Son: I could see why dad only wrestled versus box. He had a wired physic with some decent muscle on him. He wasn't built like a boxer. And with him leaving a double life. It wouldn't be like him to be punching people in the face then hanging out with them afterwards. Wouldn't work to well for him. BUT wrestling. Yup. It's contact without being aggressive. Your rolling around with squirrely moves that pin people. They tap out and everyone is cool with it. It's a show of whose the best wrestler verses how can I knock this person out cold.

Son: Yup. I'm avoiding any of the details in this book and will leave all the sobering "I got in trouble" details in his next book. This way, it portrays him as he was. Then the dark side version will be about his double life. By reading them in separate accounts, you'll see it like I saw it, from my perspective... after my mom dumped all those secrets on me.

Son: Me loving my mom and thought she was awesome as well; it was the least I could do for her. She taught me so much; she took care of me and didn't have anyone to go to. Seriously. She was trying to pursue religion through christianity, but it didn't get the same results. Dad was good at what he did, so he would go to church with her. Just another cover.

Son: It must be my purpose, because I listen sincerely and personalize what they are saying. To the point when I gave her a reply back; it was supportive of her and offered some solutions. Mom, I'll talk to dad with soft intros. Like: Dad, moms' really pissed at you and she would like you to go to church with her this coming Sunday. He would say ok. I became like the *live-in* marriage counselor. It wouldn't be 24/7. It would be far and in between.

Son: Ok. I got to stop writing about this or I won't have anything for the next book. Lol. It will take away from this one. And would be two perspectives laced with survival tips. Two themes woven together will confuse the reader and won't be able to grasp these two sides, the way I did and everyone else at the time.

Son: Oops a daisy. One spoiler on my mom. She was convinced for a season to be like him. She reasoned with me, the only other alternative to her was suicide. Divorce was NOT an option back then. It wasn't an option in the legal system. *It was horrible to see her pain out in the open now,* with all the details she shared with me about dad.

Son: I think it was meant to be for me to get a real-life example on how women are treated in society. Then I ended up later, being a single parent father. I choose not to remarry and gave my children all of me, when I came home after work. It was a priceless experience. I had to be a dad at times, then have the sensitivity to be a mom at times.

Son: Between the two experiences of understanding my dad's and mom's marriage – can't get a divorce and my marriage when divorce became legal. I saw "the stuck with this person life" and "the holy bananas they just left me" out in the cold life. Dang. No option like my mother: she had to work it out, to mine – left me-cold. I'm gone. Completely the opposite of each other experiences.

Son: Me looking back, single parenting was priceless. I would do it all over again, without blinking an eye. *Why put up with all the fakeness?* Seeing it on both sides now, it's allowed me to look at relationships in a deeper way. When the times right; I will be helping women know within fives minutes, if the guy she's interested in, is a good choice and worth the effort in connecting with him. This will be a game changer.

15. I did what I wanted to do as a Teenager. Hopefully they'll find something they like to do. Most change several times before they find something. I didn't like farming, so I left home and restored a greenhouse for one year rent free. Got ready for business. Hired heavy set guy five feet five inches. One hundred eighty-two pounds. Chewed tobacco. He could spit. I told him to quit spitting, there are women around here. Eighteen to nineteen people working for me. Guy was from a neighboring town. Good worker. Nobody took greenhouse over when I left. Sold flowers at farmer's market. Green house gives you a break in winter. Good summer job.

Son: Dad did. Dad dropped out of school when he was sixteen. And started selling gladiolas at the Farmer's Market and at a the cross roads of a busy location. He sold enough, to buy a run-down greenhouse in a near by local city. Another good traffic area.

Son: The run-down green house had a broken-down furnace in it. His dad knew of someone who could fix it. Bam. Dad's farm experience in growing plants, kicks in. He was selling so many plants, he's hiring almost twenty people to help him run it. *Hmm.* And dad did not even graduate high school. This was before HR Departments, etc. Amazing all the overhead we put into businesses today.

Son: Dad is drafted into the Korean War at the age of twenty. *Hmm.* What does he do with the Green House Business? Dad sells it and buy's mom a wedding ring. Goes to boot camp, he comes home to marry mom and the day after their honey moon is sent to Korea.

Son: Dad, didn't take weeks, months and years to make decisions. He went to the core of the challenge. Made a decision and was all in, with his decision.

Son: What's crazy, he didn't do much talking about why or why not and or have regrets. It's like he instantly sized up the situation and knew what was best for him, his now wife and his family.

Son: This goes back to all those other tips; that he is letting us know, to have a more enriching life. And increase the odds of surviving our hell and back moments.

17. Got to hang on the Tiger's Tail. Cuz, I know he can pull you around and get you out of trouble.

Son: Lol. Who is that one person, that's going to be your tiger? I forgot all about this tip. *Seriously.*

Son: Knowing dad, this could be his reference about getting in trouble with one of his friends, that lived about two miles from him. *Maybe his friend was not only a trouble maker like him, but an escape artist as well?* They would wrestle together, was true but also maybe, in reference to them being a professional escape artists.

Son: Flip it around. No matter how dad got into trouble, he would always have an alibi to cover for him.

Son: Ok, I was letting some of the other things dad did, overshadow his wisdom as well. My apologies. Let's get back on track.

Son: No matter how scary the life situations facing us, look at the positive side. *It's hard believe-me you.* But in my personal experience with my pit bull dog, Max. My eyes were completely open to animals perceived and or told to us are vicious killers. *Is not true.*

Son: My Pitbull Max, was the sweetest dog I've ever had. He was all love. Then I began to believe, it was the dog's owners that make them vicious, by mentally bullying them all the time. To the point, they trust no one. It's messed up bad. Then working with other "wild vicious" animals. *Is all fear miss information.*

Son: All animals are good, even tigers. Sweet animals. I've seen good owners of tigers, had to leave them for a period of years. Then when the owner returns the tigers go nuts and is soooo excited to see their friend again. I've seen this with elephants, bears, gorillas in the wild and even alligators. Yup even alligators.

Son: When we approach any animals with sincere unconditional love in a peaceful way, they feel it and connect with it. Period. I learned this in baby steps because I too was apprehensive.

Son: Ok enough of the commercials.

Son: We need to take the time to learn how to gently hold onto the Tiger's tail – our hellish event that is scaring the cookies out of us – because it might be the very thing, that helps us escape. Escape a bad relationship, bad choice of employment and or any another situation in our life.

18. Being Last Born gives you the perspective of go with the flow. First thing you know, kindergarten playing, before you know your in-grade school. Get big picture upfront. Not worrying about big picture, enjoy big picture.

Son: This is deep, being acute at a very early age to being aware of the big picture of, while the rest of the family is doing things.

Son: Then this means this awareness is not seen with smaller families. Dad came from a family of nine. Seven brothers and sisters, plus two parents.

Son: This understanding doesn't kick in until the number of brother and sisters grows between the first and last child.

Son: Wow. *Did I just say that?* I just got it. Dad thank you for all these survival tips; even when you knew I wasn't grasping some of these, when you were saying them at the time. I was too busy capturing them; while dad was speaking them to me, like a ripe fruit dropping from a tree on a windy day.

Son: Not only did dad grasp this, he also embraced it, by enjoying the big picture. Now this makes a lot of sense when dad was grown up and had a family himself. He would always ask me, hey I'm going to go visit my family, you want to come. We'll stop for ice-cream on the way. Lol. *Dad would always treat me, like rewarding me to interact with his family.* All along he was showing me, he was enjoying the big picture.

Son: He connected with all of his family on a routinely basis. I would not see this with his other family members. Dad was the only one. They would have their convenient favorites, but not everyone like dad.

Son: Dad even went to the distance setting up, making plans and hosting family reunions with all of his family. And guess what he chooses as the favorite food for hosting his family's reunion? *Oh man, you guessed it.* HOME MADE **CRANKED** ICE CREAM! Everyone of his family and their families was in line to get a scoop. You should have seen all their faces with smiles.

Son: Which set them up for the **BIG** Family Reunion **Picture**s.

Son: How did you like the full circle of dad saying, set back and enjoy the Big Picture?

21. Think to Do Good. If you raise hell it's going to slow you down in your activities. Very easy to get into trouble.

Son: Here again, Dad is somewhat admitting, he has a getting into trouble addiction. Lol.

Son: While admitting it, if you got things to do with deadlines; then it's a REAL good idea not to tempt hellish events, on one's life.

Son: Now if an unplanned hellish event happens in one's life, then it's easier to think of a good outcome from it. Due to not being the one, who actually instigated it.

Son: The one who instigated the hellish event, is focused on thinking bad towards someone. With this mindset, this individual is NOT going to accomplish much in their lives.

Son: The one who is focused on thinking about good things happening is one's life. With this mindset, this individual has increased their odds in accomplishing much in their lives.

22. Do Something Good. Helps them stay out of trouble, stay out of jail.

Son: This locks in the last one #21. Once I think of something good, then I need to do that good thing. This locks in thinking and doing something good.

Son: Then repeat think and do something good. Keep doing it, like dad said earlier, until it becomes automatically natural. This sets up the heart/mindset to extra time, to think and be ready to react in a hellish event.

So: It's like a cheap insurance policy; that the person won't have time to do something bad, because they've now become addicted to doing good.

Son: The Doing Good Addiction feeds on itself. All the good results that person is attaining; are like pats on the back, to keep doing good.

23. Go Where You Have to Go and Take it Slow and Easy. If you rush into stuff, you usually get into trouble, make a mistake.

Son: Faster doesn't automatically mean better.

Son: There are too many variables that could cause a different result.

Son: Odds are high that the person who is rushing through something is; they really don't want to do it but they have to. Thinking "the quicker I do this, the quicker I'm done."

Usually this is associated with having no experience in doing stuff. Period.

Son: Slow Means More. And Faster Means Less. Yup 3.0

Son: Slow and steady, this way I can make adjustments through the process of getting stuff done quicker.

Son: Less Means More. The way I can make this work is take a few minutes and think about the stuff I want to get done. Strategize. *Strategy is half the process* and everything else will fall into place.

Son: Choose the least amount of stuff that needs to get done, THAT WILL MAKE THE **BIGGEST** IMPACT. Seriously.

Son: Example: I need to remodel my interior of my home. A gallon of paint is one of the cheapest cost items, in helping me remodel my home interior. I pick a light color grey for the walls. The light grey color will make everything else pop in the room, like it's a completely new to the room.

Son: I personally know this. I did it to my interior and I was blown away how everything came alive again. I got a ton of compliments and only cost me $45.00 at that time. Less means more.

Son: I had a double kicker. In the past, I would tape off the areas so that "I wouldn't get paint on them." But with this tip, I didn't buy painter's tape. Saved money and time, that it took to tape everything off. I went slower at the edges of painting around trims, plates and etc. This not rushing; allowed me to save money and a lot of time, not ripping the tape off and making touch ups. At worst the tape would stick to items and or rip some paint off. I would have to go back and scrap the paint off and repaint around the edges. It made it a more enjoyable experience. Versus dreading the cleanup and touch up process in the end.

Son: This got me thoroughly hooked on Less is More and Slow is Faster. Thank You Dad for that tip. Priceless.

24. Enjoy Today. Best thing to do. Go to fast you get into trouble. Least you'll be out of troubles.

Son: This is the other side of the last tip 23.

Son: Understanding and Harnessing the benefits of Less is More and Slow is Faster. Allows me to be more relaxed to enjoy the process.

Son: I own the process versus the process owning me.

Son: This strategy allows me to enjoy today, at it's fullest.

Son: If something goes wrong in the process then I'll have more time to adjust to it versus compound the time to getting it done.

27. It's Ok to be Embarrassed When We Fall Down. Can't help it. If able get right back up.

Son: If it happens then it happened. There's nothing I can do, to go back and change those results.

Son: Accept it. *Even laugh at it.* The more I can relax about it, the more I can focus to recoup from it. Versus spending all my mental energy on being embarrassed by it. Use that mental energy on recouping, to recoup better.

29. It would be nice if We Could put Everything in a Bag, Shake it up and whatever falls out; do it.

Son: Lol. This is all dad. Wit and humor at the same time, to make a profound statement.

Son: Working full time, husband, father, building the next home for us to live in, playing with us, maintenance, yard chores and fixing random unplanned problems. At times, these were all firing on all cylinders. *And needed to be addressed* **NOW**.

Son: With that, dad says this tip.

Son: It would be a game changer; if we could put all Got to Doers Nowers into a bag. Shake it to see what falls out. Then just focus on that one; while all the other Got to Doers Nowers understand and will be patiently waiting their turns.

Son: **BECAUSE...** That's the rules to the... Hop in Bag and Shake It Game! 😊

39. Start Your Day Working and Finish Your Day Working. Gets the blood flowing. Paces yourself. Somedays might not have anything to do; that's when you can take a vacation. Brings things up to speed.

Son: This is the other half of the; work hard, play hard and sleep hard tip.

Son: It takes practice getting into the heart/mind set of starting your day working. Most of us like to start out with something easy to do, then maybe something harder latter in the day.

Son: Remember, my dad started his day out Milking cows; at the age of five.

Son: Some of us have jobs that require us to start working in the morning. That gets the blood moving too. I had a start real early in the morning job for 45 years. Yup. Sobering. So, I can personally see how this tip is beneficial. My blood was flowing to the point; I was planning on working on projects, when I got home.

Son: Now, we find ourselves with no projects to work on. This sets us up, to take some time off and relax. Which in turn, makes our vacations much better and appreciated. Versus, *oh...* it's just another vacation.

Son: Harnessing Getting into our work and or projects, automatically produces us to get into our vacations.

Son: Which in turn balances out our lives.

50. Choose Jobs Based on Your Likes so that You will like your job. I liked freedom so I picked and outside job.

Son: Not at first with dad. He had to learn this from personal experience. However, he didn't drag this process out. Within a few weeks to a few months; he was jumping boat, to swim to another boat.

Son: Dad like to do a variety of projects inside and outside our homes, while completing them in a timely manner.

Son: No one ever had to motivate him to do anything. Period.

Son: He dropped out of high school. And started his flower shop business.

Son: After he came home from the Korean War, being married, he had to get a job. A big auto manufacturing plant was in the next town over, so he got a job there. Basically, stand in one spot on an assembly line. This was driving dad nuts, so he transferred to another job within the auto manufacturer. Nope. Didn't work either.

Son: Hmm. Dad was in fork in the road decision time. He needed a job; but the one he had, he hated it. When everyone else thought it was a great job, with great pay.

Son: Dad decided to jump that job of isolation, to work for the local utility company. He was outside working on different jobs throughout different communities. A new job location every day. If there were bad storms then he would be on the same job, for a few days.

Son: From digging ditches to laying power lines, to reading meters and finishing his utility career in the gas department.

Son: The gas department gave him the most variety. The utility company had 24 shifts. They started a new shift on every hour; to have fresh workers starting routinely, through out the work day. Incase random problems that would pop up, they would have a new fresh team to work on it. It was brilliant. This was perfect for dad. Dad loved his variety of outside getter doners.

Son: To keep all those 24 shifts from getting into a "boring" routine, the company changed their start times every two weeks. So, if dad's start time was 6 am then in two weeks, his start time could be 2 pm. Two weeks later, his start time could be 10pm. Dad loved this like no other. He would pull out his 24-hour gas department time sheets every once in a while, to show me his new schedule. Priceless to see his face smiling, when he was going through the motions of showing me.

Son: Dad's saying. Be honest with ourselves; in knowing who we really are and match that up with a job that's like that, or closely related to it. When we do this, we are going to be more-happier at doing our jobs. This in turn, effects everything else in our lives.

Son: Almost forgot to mention. Dad loved reading home meters so much; that he was done with his required list, with five hours of an eight-hour shift. So, he would find a local church pew and take a three-hour nap.

Son: Word got out that dad was "sleeping" on the job. His boss was pissed and was going to reprimand dad. But since dad was apart of the union, they couldn't without first investigating it.

Son: Dad was smiling when he got his schedule list of meters to read, hopped into his utility truck. His boss hopped in as well. Dad studies the list, strategizes the layout and heads out to start. Dad stops at community location and starts reading meters.

Son: As dad is doing this, his boss says your starting in the wrong location for this list. His boss was needling everything dad was doing.

Son: Dad says to his boss, *Arre you watching me what I do on my job* or are you telling me how to do my job?

Son: His boss was silent. *I'm telling you.* Dad says, *have you ever done this job?* His boss says, *no.*

Son: Dad says, *then watch me.*

Son: When dad started this metering job; he realized that the patterns the company set up, was not the most efficient. So.

he would read the meters in the most efficient way to get a three-hour break at the end of his shift EVERY day.

Son: Once dad was done in five hours, his boss verified every meter was read and dad actually was done in five hours. Dad's boss was speechless. His boss had no grounds to reprimand him.

Son: Dad's boss asked him, *why don't you take the easy way and do it in our pattern?* Dad said, *your way isn't easy, it's frustrating doing all this double backing. My way is smooth and makes a more effective work day.*

Son: Again, dad's boss was speechless. Day done.

Son: Dad's boss went back to his office and reset up all meter reading list to dad's more efficient routine.

Son: The whole meter reading work force was now pissed at dad, for making them all work "harder." Reading more meters for the same pay. And dad lost his three-hour nap time, at the nearest local church.

Son: Dad's satisfaction was two-fold. *First.* The co-workers who ratted on him; for sleeping on the job at the nearest church. Now had to work harder, every day, week, month and year. FOR THE SAME PAY. Priceless. *Second.* Dad could stay busy working which he loved to do, knowing he was going to get better sleep at night, without him having his three-hour nap time. Lol.

Son: The Utility company started to realize how much dad was loving being efficient – no matter what job he was on, they wanted to make him a Shift Manager. Dad said no.

Son: They were disappointed and asked why? Dad said, *I love to work versus sitting around telling others what to do.* This was priceless. Dad was basically telling his bosses in a nice way; your lazy and should be ashamed of yourselves for getting higher pay, then those who are actually doing the work. This is classic dad. Saying things in witty and deep ways, but not being in your face offensive. *Priceless 4.0*

Son: Ok, in closing. The workers that were totally pissed at dad; for making them work harder for their eight hours, actually set them up to getting better raises. They had the proof; as to why they should get a better raise, based on all of their increased production rates. The company couldn't argue with it, because it was all documented; with the amount of meters being read per day.

Son: As a result, we as a family had a summer of welfare food for dad being on strike, but it was worth it for dad. AND we had bunch of new priceless experiences from it.

55. Have No Regrets. I have no regrets. If something doesn't work out, then that's what was supposed to happen. Try two to three times and doesn't work out then that's what was to be. Best thing to do is keep on mind and you can always go back to it or accept that's the best it gets.

Son: This was demonstrated in Dad's last tip we went into depth with. Plus; all the other ones related to it.

Son: Dad realized early on; we waste a lot of time hoping and trying different approaches only to get frustrated at it. So instead of repeating that cycle and wasting time, just let it go. Upfront. Nip it in the rearend. Don't eliminate it. Just tuck up in our minds, for a possible solution later on. Or, it was meant to be nothing more than that.

Son: This was the staple in everything dad did and experienced. Even during his unplanned hellish moments, that consumed his life.

Son: This is one of dad's strongest tips in having a more enriching life with himself, his wife, his family and everything else in his life. Period.

Son: We Except it. We Don't walk away from it; we just tuck it in our minds for a possible solution in the future. For now, we just keep moving forward with our lives.

60. No Matter who Starts a Fight, will get Tired Out and Stop.

Son: This is interesting. Dad never picked fights, even though he was getting into trouble a lot. The people who got pissed off at dad, was because he did something to them. Which they had every right too. But would soon realize with dad's friendly demeanor, they would eventually get tired of justifying being pissed off and stop.

Son: Sometimes mom would be so pissed off at dad, she would start throwing things at him. Sometimes she would miss him, hit him and or he would catch them with a smile on his face. Yup. She must have loved him; because the objects she-choose to throw, were not considered dangerous.

Son: Dad with his classic friendly demeanor would stand there and be supportive to what mom was trying to say.

Son: After ten to twenty minutes of intense yelling, she would tire out and stop. Every time. To continue her being pissed, even though she's tired out, would walk out of the house and down the road! Me, being a kid and watching this, would say to dad... *dad we need to go get mom!* Dad would always reply back... *she'll be back.*

Son: It's amazing how dad had the wisdom to know; even if he was in the right, would let the person vent away. Knowing they'll get tired out AND... AND... the conversation will end a WHOLE LOT faster. Versus getting caught up in the drama and dragging it out longer.

Son: Summary. Fights are Like Fires. The fire will keep burning, as long as wood and gasoline are added to it. That simple.

Son: Stop throwing wood on the fire and it will go out. Stop throwing gasoline on the fire and it will go out. Period.

Son: Dad's friendly confident supportive demeanor was what attracted mom to come back. After mom thought about how she handled the situation, she felt guilty and return home. All because dad wouldn't get caught up in the drama, while mom was being pissed off.

65. Holidays Make Good Breaks.

Son: By not having to go to work; dad's work hard, play hard and sleep hard routines could take a break. BUT.

Son: BUT... dad was addicted to them. He still was up early and working on something. I remember all to well as a kid, trying to sleep in on Saturday morning. ZZZZZZZZZZ. The sounds of an electric saw cutting wood at 7am. Yup. That was my alarm clock for several years on the weekends. Got so use to it, and it wouldn't wake me up anymore.

Son: A couple of times, I would crawl out of bed to go see dad and ask him why he can't wait. When I got where he was working. I asked him... *why?* In dad's classic style, would say... *you here to help me out? Hand me that tape measure.* I would hand him the tape measure then go back to bed. After a couple of times, I stopped asking. Lol

Son: Dad did enjoy the holiday breaks because he had an extra nine hours, to his day. Dad chose to get his everyday after working home chores, done first thing in the morning. He keeps his; start your day working and end your day working routine. While having an extra nine hours with his family.

Son: Dad love to play hard, especially with family. It was Priceless. Dad was the energy of the family. Mom was very supportive of that energy. They were like a Swiss watch working together. There was little talk, if any at all. It's like they read each other's minds while what they were doing.

Son: Looking back and having children myself; if dad did leave the family, there would have been ZERO energy in our family to keep it going. *Seriously.*

67. Always Have Time for Your Favorite Recreation.

Son: This is the other half of tip 65.

Son: Most the time, dad had his weekends, until he started working for the gas department. But that was after us kids move out and on with our lives.

Son: Dad and mom would capitalize on the weekends; right down to the minute, dad punched out on Fridays. Lol. Yup.

Son: During the late spring and summer months; Mom would have everything packed up in the car and ready to go to the cabin.

Son: It gets better.

Son: To save money; dad would hitch hike a ride to work, with his work buddy. To save time; Mom would drive us and packed car to pick dad up, at clock out time.

Son: Drive straight to the cabin, with a dinner pitstop half way there.

Son: The cabin was dad's and mom's favorite recreation. They took it soooo seriously that no one could talk about; politics, religion and any other news item of the day. They made it clear; we were all there to have a relaxing, restful fun time. Without being obnoxious. Anyone who was, found out fast to stop or leave. This set the tone to always wanting to be at the cabin, any chance we could get.

Son: The scenery on the cabin lakeview was surreal, inviting and addictive. All you had to do was sit on the porch and or in the yard, lakeview side, and you forgot about all your concerns and problems. You could see it on everyone's faces. **Priceless 5.0**

68. When Someone Makes Fun of You and You Don't Like It, You Take It. Let Them Think It Doesn't Bother You.

Son: What can I say more? If you decided to read this book cover to cover then you would know by now; this has been dad's common theme, in dealing with confrontations.

Son: Another new example: On weekends during fall, winter and early spring; my mom's sisters with their husbands would get together and play cards. Mom had three sisters. That would be the eight of them sitting at the table. And this would mean, it was the gals against the guys.

Son: They would sit, gal guy, gal guy, etc.; all the way around the table.

Son: The gals took their card playing seriously, why the guys would enjoy the game.

Son: My dad and my mom's sister, were the comedians at the card table. They all be busting out loud laughing throughout every game they played; I stopped playing with my cousins, just to be with the laughter.

Son: They would play the same game until they got bored with it, then choose a whole different game to liven them all back up again.

Son: Ok, back to the gals taking the game seriously. At times they would make verbal cheap shots at my dad and other guys. Dad wouldn't react to it other than with a respectful smile. This would make the gals step up their game and play even harder.

Son: Then at the right time, when the gals would get mad at other. To the point; they would stand up and start yelling at each other's faces. Dad in his classic way of delivery; would say a witty and humorous comment, related to what the gals were yelling about. The gals would stop yelling. Look at dad and bust out laughing. Then their funny sister would make a similar funny comment as well. The two gals then would sit back down and start playing cards again like nothing ever happened.

Son: Dad and her sister were the main comedians of the greater family. Yet all of them would say funny things at times.

Son: That was the main reason, why I looked forward to watching them play cards. It was extremely entertaining and informative.

70. Stay Away from Pranks. That's not REAL fun; fake fun.

Son: Lol. Ok dad.

Son: Dad was like king of the pranksters.

Son: As he got older, the people around him started to think nothing about his pranks. And just ignore him.

Son: So, dad had to *up his game* in having fun with people. This is where dad started to hone his wit and humorous comments. People were laughing and enjoying his style of delivery. Getting people to sincerely laugh and enjoy his witty humor, became addictive to dad. This stayed with dad the rest of his life. No matter who he was around; people enjoyed his humor, even the first timers out in public settings.

71. There's Always a Kid Out There Who Wants to Race.

Son: I don't remember any stories dad told about racing with someone.

Son: The only thing that comes to mind; would be, there is always someone out there in the world that says they are and or tries to be better than you.

Son: Or it was just an observance thing on his part. Noticing no matter what your doing and or not doing, some one will always want to race you. Which a person could waste a lot of time, just thinking and trying to out race everyone and everywhere. Your life is still in the same spot, so why race. What does it prove? You wasted a lot of time racing?

Son: Then it could also mean; there's people out their that will deliberately, want to get our minds racing about different issues. Hoping to get our minds to crash and burn, like a bad race car accident. *Interesting.* Didn't think about that. Thank you, dad for this tip! *It just sunk in.*

92. Being Spoiled Straightens Us Out. It Ends Up Helping Us Understand What's Really Important.

Son: It gives the illusion that this is what life really is like. Not realizing that I'm lazy and have no clue to what others are doing for me, so I can live this illusionary life.

Son: If I'm ever awaken from my illusionary life; then I realize quickly the price others have paid, for me to live in a fantasy world. If I receive that then I look for a job, that I can start learning how to take care of myself. Thereafter, I will never take things for granted.

Son: If I become bitter and angry from being awaken to reality, then it reveals to me how lazy I really am. I will look for others and or ways that I can use to keep my illusion alive. I rather stay lazy then work. I believe in being lazy so much, that I'm entitled to being lazy. I *will* never appreciate anything in my life.

94. If You Want to Travel be Smart about It – Look Out for Yourself.

Son: My dad love to travel. And mom loved traveling with dad… to the point…

Son: When dad retired from the utility company, they bought a place down in warm southern state, where mom's mother lived.

Son: Once Christmas was in the books, they were on their way to the warm state for the Winter months.

Son: They would go on cruises, go site seeing and for a change of scenery; travel to see friends that lived in other states.

Son: They bought a just get by modest place to live in, so that they would have more money to travel with.

Son: It was fitting for them, for all the hellish seasons they went through. It was like a pat on the back, for surviving all those storms from hell together.

Son: In those travels, they learned to stay to themselves. Versus being that friendly couple, when they were around family and friends. After a few close calls; they learned fast it's a cheap travel insurance policy, to take the approach in not trusting anyone.

Son: Discovering the vulnerabilities of being far away from home. Can be sobering at times. Help is so far away. Limited resources. PLUS trying to ignore that, so that I and or we can have a "good" time traveling.

96. Only Take the Advice from People Who Experienced What You Have Experienced.

Son: Dad learned this early on. Getting up every morning before six am to milk cows; helping with farm chores, at the age of five. Yup. He said he was so small, he had to sit on a bucket to milk the cows. Lol.

Son: So, with his work ethics at age five, dad would only take advice from those who actually had proof of work.

Son: What's funny and ironic at the same time; is the people who have zero experience are the ones giving everyone else their "priceless" advice. Where in fact, they have zero experience and are just clueless spreaders. You know, like the manure spreaders on the farms. But the manure spreaders on the farm are actually doing something good for the farm. Whereas these clueless spreaders are making the people who listen to them, into clueless zombies.

Son: It's like a mother or dad of a child, who never put the time into raising their child. Period. Abandons the family due to being self-centered. Actually, it's the best thing for the family. The self-centered mindset is toxic to any family. Personally speaking.

Son: So now later in the child's life; that child has children themselves. At one point the child reaches out to the abandon parent who was never in their life. Talking to them about their child, which is the abandon's parent's grandchild, to try to reconnect.

Son: But the abandon parent always talks to their kid, like they have no clue on how to raise a kid. And their doing it *ALL* wrong. At first the child of the abandon parent, takes it personal. But later realizes their abandon parent, was never there for them and never raised a child themselves. So, the child of the abandon parent is now at a fork in the road relationship with their abandon parent.

Son: Now the child of the abandon parent makes the decision; not to connect with the abandon parent, to keep their sanity.

Son: Summary. Let actions speak louder than words.

Son: When someone starts offering advice like items on clearance at a store... lol ... then ask yourself... *while they are talking to you...* do they have any tangible proof that they actually did it themselves? Or did they just do "a lot of studying" so that makes them "specialists" in their field, of who knows what. If they have no tangible evidence then they truly don't know jack, about what they are talking about.

Son: Oh, this procedure works great. Did they actually go through the procedure and get the personal results they needed? If no then don't listen. Research deeper yourself versus talking their word on it.

Son: Ok. In my dad's case. He actually built a house from the ground up, with very little assistance. Sure, he had someone dig the whole in the ground, so that he could lay the foundation himself. He did all his carpentry, electrical, plumbing, roofing and finishing himself. Yup. With very little assistance. Other than mom helping with the finishing work.

Son: Once dad got the home to the finishing next phase, mom was in drooling everyday season.

Son: Conclusion. Dad would only take advice from people who actually worked on homes like he did. They both can relate to each other.

Son: Oops. One more conclusion. The child of the abandon parent: only takes advice on how to raise a child, from a parent who was abandon by their parent as well. Or second best, by another single parent.

‡ Relationships Survival Tips ‡
QTY 21

4. Pick Good Friends. It's Easier When You Have a Good Mother and Father. They want somebody to be with. If two different personalities; won't stay together very long.

Son: The younger someone is, the harder it is to find a good friend. Most of us are so innocently trying to make friends; with anyone that looks interested in having a conversation with us, on a consistent basis. But it's more than that.

Son: Then if I'm so desperate to have a friend, I settle for someone who has a different personality then I do. It's like I justify the contrast, as to them being unique.

Son: Dad recognizes this as a problem for younger people. And the only thing that's going to help balance this out, is if by chance the children have good parents. Good parents will take the time to give their children examples of what a good friend is. And how to cut down all the unnecessary drama; time wasters, by avoiding bad friends.

Son: Good parents would point out. Do you have the same interests/likes? Then give examples. When you disagree, do you both get frustrated and stop talking to each other for a while? Then give examples what good friends would do.

Does one make messes and the other cleans them all up, all the time? Then give examples about accountability. Etc.

Son: *A Double Plus* in Picking a Good Friend. If by chance I can master picking a good friend when I'm younger; then it will increase my odds in picking a good spouse, in the future.

5. Stay Single. Never get the idea of chasing women or men or getting married. Some get married right away without being single first. So that if I'm single one day, I'll be at peace with it.

Son: Lol. Ok dad 2.0 … Dad was no angel. But mom did captivate him enough, to where he wanted to be with her all the time. To the point, he married her when she was seventeen. Yup. He had to get her dad's consent, since she was a minor. Back then this was appropriate.

Son: So, dad was one of those who got married right away, without being single first.

Son: And this is that point, where dad found himself, when his free movie sweet heart passed on before he did. He was extremely lonely being by himself. He lived a little more than four years, after she passed on.

Son: I would visit him often to help him get through his loneliness, without her. His world revolved around her 24/7. Which made it extra special and they had a lot of enriching memories together.

Son: When I visit him regularly, I would notice her pictures all over the place, in every room of their home. He was defiantly missing her.

Son: He never really found peace in being by himself. He had to be around someone, who cared about him.

Son: So, during those a little more than four years of loneliness; he realizes couples should wait to get married, versus rushing right into it. The couple should be looking at their relationship, in a longer healthier view for both of them. That way if either one; passes on before the other, they will both be more at peace with themselves and each other. *That's pretty deep.*

Son: I ended up falling in my dad's footsteps, but waited a tad longer before getting married. Long story short. She divorced me out of the blue, in a few years later. Me never being single that young, was devastated and I took it hard. It took several years to toughen up and move on. Now looking back, I will never regret having my children, but I should have waited a few more years. Versus jumping into the relationship blindly.

Son: Ok. Confession time over. I was double emphasizing, what dad had experienced personally. Oh dang. Maybe that's what dad was referring to as well, because he witnessed my situation first hand.

Son: *Ok one more.* I did end up becoming at peace with myself, a few years later when I got custody of my children. She moved out of state and I stayed here. So, she had to by law, give me custody of my children. But *I never remarried*, just to have someone else in my life to help me raise my children? I was so at peace with myself being single; that I embraced being a single parent dad, with all of my heart. It was priceless and would do it all over again, **without blinking an eye.**

7. When We're Married, We have Several Bosses. Most women like to boss. Man thinks he's the boss but he's fooling himself.

Son: Lol. Dad hit the nail on the head with this one. I witnessed it first-hand, living in dad's home while growing up.

Son: Regardless how dad's demeanor was, wit, working a day job, building the next home to live in, playing hard with the family; it didn't matter. Mom got her way.

Son: It's not that dad was mom's butler; mom was sincerely looking at all the angles. She would logically be embracing what was necessary to do for the family.

Son: Then mom had a way of explaining it to dad, where dad would say, that makes sense to me, let's do it.

Son: Again, it wasn't mom being a persuasive arguer. It was dad, would be focusing on the family's future needs and mom was focusing on the family's current needs.

Son: When mom wanted to insist on making future decisions on family needs, she would end up agreeing with dad. Dad did the same logical reasoning with mom, so she could understand at a deeper level as to why.

Son: Dad was keen enough to recognize this in the beginning. So, he accepted it versus being stubborn and insisting he got his way ... *BECAUSE HE WAS THE BOSS.*

Son: By dad learning how to listen to mom; when she was bringing to dad's attention, the current needs of the family. Dad did this repeatedly to the point; it set mom up, to be willing to listen to dad about the family's future needs.

34. Let Your Companion Say What They Need to Say and Just Listen. So won't make the same mistake.

Son: This is dad's growth process, after the last tip 7.

Son: Just letting your companion talk is way the opposite of actually listening to their details.

Son: Then at the respectable moments, respond back with what they are saying – in your own words. Simple Example: Your partner says we need to do A, B and C. After a while of sincerely listening to them, you say... *That makes sense, we need to do a, b and c.*

Son: Better communication, means increasing your odds in getting through a hellish event easier.

Son: Better communication; means enjoying enriching moments together, in a deeper way. Easier.

35. If Your Spouse Wants to Leave Let them. You'll find out How Much They Really Love You.

Son: I thought dad was crazy, when I was learning this while growing up in dad's house.

Son: Mom would get so pissed off at dad at times, she would leave the house, with the loud sounds of a slamming door behind her. That loud BAM resonated in my heart big time. My mom was my everything. She helped me conquered kids laughing at me, in third grade.

Son: I would look dad in the eyes and say *go after her dad, we need her.* He would look into my eyes with even deeper peace and say... *no.*

Son: I was devastated. How could dad say that, if he really loved her?

Son: Dad was wise. He let the silence kick in. Then said ... *If you truly love someone, then you'll give them the space to leave. If they truly love you then they will come back.*

Son: After a few hours, mom did come back.

Son: Mom did this few more times. As I got older in my mid-teens and more confident; one time I had to go after her myself. Dad never stopped me either.

Son: Once I caught up to mom; she was sitting under the overpass creek bridge, just down from the farm.

Son: *Mom, you need to come back home. We love you. We need you...* She looked me in the eyes and said she can't take it anymore. She needs a break. *Please let me be son... I need some quiet alone time.* Silence. *I'll be back home. I just need some time.* I gave mom a hug, told her I love her. And soberly left.

Son: When I got back to the house, I let dad know what mom said. He looked at me with the eyes of *this is what true love is all about.*

Son: It was a few days later, I encouraged mom to vent her frustrations about dad. And I'll just listen. So, every school day afterwards, when I got home off the bus. I was sitting next to mom's sewing machine; listening to mom's frustrations, while she was sewing clothes for us, etc.

Son: *What's crazy,* looking back. My ex left me and never came back. I was waiting for her, like my dad was for my mother. The difference was my ex never came back.

Son: If I would have applied this tip to my own life experience then I would of know at the moment, she truly didn't love me. I would have moved on quicker versus waiting a few more years.

Son: *Note to Self*: Self-Centered people do not engage in relationships. They use relationships for themselves. If that person is self-centered to the core; from the tips of their toes to the tip of their heads, they will never truly love anyone. They are in love with themselves. Themselves and only themselves.

36. Give Your Spouse Room to let them do What They want to do. Don't want to tie them down all the time. So, they can be themselves.

Son: This was dad's taking the tip 35 to a deeper level.

Son: Mom ended joining a bowling team with her sisters, to play in bowling tournaments. Working out at the spa with her sisters.

Son: She ended up getter closer to her sisters. To the point, they were sharing similar experiences about their husbands. This comforted mom, knowing she wasn't crazy or alone in her relationship with dad.

41. Learn How to Have a Family. Getting the chance of knowing the purpose of being the head of family. See how the children work together.

Son: Growing up in a family, is different then having a family. However, it does make the process balanced and complete. If and only if I want to. If I don't want to then I truly don't love family or myself. *That's Deep.*

Son: If I love being a part of growing up in the family then I'm going to love learning how to be head of the family, with my companion.

Son: Dad got to see this from being the last born, in a family of nine. While being the youngest; he was seeing the flow of the family and the big picture of the family. Which in his words, he was able to enjoy the big picture.

Son: Dad was able to take this experience with him, in being head of the house now.

Son: Now it's, switching from playing with one of his brothers and or sisters, while enjoying the big picture. To how are the children interacting with each other in the big picture?

Son: Another one of dad's tips sinking in deeper. *If a parent really wants to be a parent, they are going to want to learn how to be a good parent.* Versus being a tyrant.

Son: Dad's deep thought kicker is... what is my purpose in being my child's parent? What is our unique connection; that makes our life journey together as parent and child more enriching. *That's so deep, I'm not adding anymore to it. Just take a few quiet minutes to **let that absorb into your spirit, mind and body...***

42. Learn How to Raise a Family. Might be for more than one reason. Might not want a big family

Son: This is deeper than the last tip 41.

Son: It doesn't stop at learn how to walk, eating on your own, potty training and connecting with family.

Son: Personally, speaking as a single parent father; learning how to raise a family, takes the whole cycle of being a grandparent to your children's children. Before your child enters into a deeper relationship with you as a parent.

Son: My children when they got in their teens was making it very clear; I was showing favoritism and wasn't a good parent. I listened. Just about like my dad with my mom.

Son: While I was listening, I was thinking ok. You'll get it when your raising your own children. You'll come back and say... *you were right dad.*

Son: One by one, as they were having their own children and a few years into trying to raise them. They would stop by or call me to say ... *dad. I'm sorry for how I treated you and said all those mean things to you. You raised three of us on your own with no help. I don't know how you did it. Thank you for putting up with me.*

Son: This is when raising my children kicked in, at a much deeper level.

Son: So, we never stop raising our children in that sense. Raising children isn't like; producing a product on an assembly line factory. Doing a one last time inspection on it, before it goes out into the world somewhere. That's cold. That's impersonal.

Son: They are unique humans. Always growing in their awareness of life and in their life journey with all of creation. Together.

Son: As they grow older and perhaps have children of their own, we will need to listen even deeper. Just as we were there with them; when they were taking their first baby steps. We will need to be there with them, when they are taking their first baby steps in learning how to be a good parent themselves. It's the same exact heart/mind set.

Son: Dad's last point on this tip. Maybe consider having a smaller family.

Son: That's funny dad said that, because earlier he said, it's good to have a big family. So, everyone can see the big picture.

Son: But now dad going full circle; he's seeing that we don't take enough time getting to know our children, in a deeper way. They get kind of lost in the "crowd."

Son: It goes along the line of less is more. But then again, it doesn't go for a parent who is self-centered. No matter the size of the family, that parent will never connect with their children in a deep way. Period.

Son: What makes more sense; after raising my three children by myself, and listening over and over all of dad's childhood stories *iiiiiiiiis...* if possible, having children farther apart versus every 2 to 3 years apart.

Son: Example. Having children every 5 to 7 years apart. This allows us as parents to enjoy a deeper relationship with our children from the age of 0 to 5 years old. Those are the priceless years; enjoying all their first timers, with lesser distractions. *Sign me up.*

Son: By 5 their more independent and helpful at doing things on their own. Now introduce having another child/sibling will be less stressful. Because the first child can take care more of themselves. And they'll even want to help mommy and daddy, with their new baby sibling. *Sign me up 2.0*

Son: Now the oldest is about 10 and the second child is about 5. They are more independent and helpful, at helping each other do things together and or on their own. Now it's time to introduce having another child/sibling, will be a whole lot less stressful then having the second child. Now you'll have two children that will want to help mommy and daddy, with their new baby sibling. *Sign me up 3.0*

Son: Ok. By now you get the idea. This seems to be a hybrid form of having children all at once and or having big families. I'm getting so excited about this new approach to having a family, I want to have another family to test this out. 😊

Son: One last thought on this new having family idea. We need to take the "I'm getting to old. Or I will be to old" ideas out of our hearts and heads. *Period.* There people on the planet, as the date I'm writing this, that are 130+ years old, some even 160+ years old and as crazy as it sounds 230+ years old. But no one talks about it, unless their apart of our daily lives.

Son: Focus on harnessing and enjoying a deeper enriching life experience with each of our children; in our life journey together, as parent and child.

45. Have Fun Having a Family. Enjoy it more.

Son: Dad. Out of all the things you tried to teach me while growing up in your home, was by your actions. Your actions spoke loud and clear, you were all in. At everything you did. Impressive. Even when you had "drunk" night with mom. Oops. But-Seriously. Yes.

Son: With dad having an "all in" heart/mind set, it was always easy for him to be in good mood to have fun anywhere anytime.

Son: Versus having to work or plan at it. The "scheduling" of a fun night or fun time, is just that. It's like the person has a magical switch, when they flip it, they automatically start having fun. That takes extra work. Setting the mood and who to hang out with. The place "looks" fun, these people are "fun" to be around. This is fake fun.

Son: Fake fun heart/mind set can be extremely moody. If the lights aren't just right, I got offended, this was a bad idea, etc.

Son: Then when I believe my fake fun is real fun long enough, eventually it gets old. And it's not fun anymore. So and so, no longer hangs out with us, a change in schedules doesn't allow the fake fun happen anymore, etc.

Son: If having an "All IN" good fun ISN'T in the heart/mind set in the beginning, then we will never enjoy it more.

Son: Mom and me was very fortunate to have dad be apart of our family. Without dad; we would have never had all the fun we had, anywhere anytime.

Son: Dad was the inspiration to knowing what life is like; when we're in an "All IN" heart/mind set, in everything, all the time. *EVEN*... when he went through all the hellish events in his life.

46. Have Fun Raising a Family. Enjoy it more

Son: Dad can't say it any better. Growing up in your house, you make it very clear to me, you were all in having fun with me, with us. Every time.

Son: Dad would blank everything else out and was 100% focused on having fun with us. Period. Phone rang, ignored it. Someone would at times try to get him to do something, he ignored them. He was all in and you could feel it in your bones.

Son: By having that real life family fun time experience with dad, now it's sobering to see some parents just going through the motions of playing with their kids. Acting like their having fun, but step out to every distraction that comes up. It's like they don't even want to play with their child.

Son: So do the child a favor, be all in when playing with them. It will last them a life time and will help them out tons; on how to play with their children.

Son: If not, they might just think having fun is going somewhere. Where in reality; the best fun is having all in fun, right where you are - with what you have. *Period.*

48. Take Your Spouse in Your Arms and Hold Them. Shows them that you love them. Naturally do it. Don't ask. Do naturally.

Son: Natural, Sensitive Timing. Priceless. One's heart needs to be naturally aware of their surroundings. People's feelings, body language and verbal tones.

Son: This tip, is an added benefit to being "ALL IN" heart/ mind set.

Son: Now when you go to hug someone, they can feel the sensitive sincerity of the hug.

Son: Verus being a quick band aid hug. *Oooo.* I like that .... *I don't want no band aid hugs from you.*

Son: And when you don't ask, *when giving a respectful hug,* it means even more.

Son: If the hug is a quick hug because you think, it means the same, as a sensitive genuine hug, then your only fooling yourself. And the person receiving it, will feel it as well.

49. Don't Look at Handicaps as Handicaps. It's something you do naturally with your spouse. Take it as it comes. If can fix, ok. If not, thank God for it.

Son: *Deep dad.*

Son: Mom ended becoming a diabetic. Dad made the adjustments in his diet, etc.; but did it naturally.

Son: He embraced it, like it was his own idea. Never looked like he was inconvenienced by mom's handicaps, as results of being a diabetic.

Son: When embracing the handicaps naturally, it makes the relationship more unique.

73. If You Find Yourself Alone Take Up Reading to Pass the Time by Easier.

Son: Dad learned this one after my mom passed on. After the reality sinked into his heart, he was REAL lonely. Mom was his 24/7.

Son: Even hanging up her pictures in every room, everywhere wasn't enough to heal the loneliness.

Son: I saw it first hand versus from afar. I actually would hang out with him on a daily basis, after mom's passing; to assist him through the process, versus by himself.

Son: So, dad took up reading, to help take his mind off the loneliness.

Son: Dad's life revolved around mom, since he was 16 years old. They were together for 67 years. And now at this point, he was 83 years old.

77. It's Good to Have Both Spouses Know How to Take Care of the Money so If One Can't the Other Can.

Son: This reality sunk in, when mom passed away.

Son: Dad always thought; the way he was "ALL IN" with everything and all those hellish events that took place in his life, the odds were stacked too high against him. He would be the first to pass on in the relationship. Dad would even talk about it often, then laugh about it.

Son: Dad was thoroughly convinced, to the point, he didn't want anything to do with setting up the will/trust either. He left that up to mom. *Period. He didn't care.*

Son: Dad would make comments, he builds and maintains the homes. And mom makes the homes livable. Then smile.

Son: It didn't take a few days after mom's passing on, to realize…. *Oh dang … where's the check book? … how did she pay the bills?* Consumed his thinking time, like no other.

Son: I had zero selfish gain in helping dad through this process, being a single parent father, *I felt sorry for him.* It was sobering to watch my dad who had his cookies together; in everything else in his life, BUT THIS.

Son: And dad feeling helpless and somewhat mad at himself, for not covering this base as well. He was so proud of himself for having 1st, 2nd and 3rd bases covered; but forgot to cover homebase.

Son: Dad didn't stay embarrassed to long. His "ALL IN" mindset kicked and was learning from me.

Son: In summary. Regardless of the reasons why I should and or can't – I need too! Period. If we want to be completely supportive of a real two-way relationship with my life partner, then we need to both take turns or together handling the bills, future planning, etc. on our finances.

Son: And this starts with just taking care of the basics handling of money; buying groceries, necessities and etc.

78. Find a Good Woman/Man. Pretty hard. Study. Still might not find anybody. They got to be willing to help each other. It's a must to get along in the beginning. If do not want to communicate, it's not going to work. Going to be miserable for rest of life. If they don't want to listen then no hope of communicating. Sorry you're going to have to go; buy them a bus ticket. They know better.

Son: Dad learned this one the painful way. It was him refusing to communicate, when mom and him were having relationship problems.

Dad: Even though dad had the "ALL IN" heart/mind set and a deep thinker, he wasn't really into deep conversations. To talk about the same topic for hours wasn't his gig.

Dad: Mom did. Mom loved to talk and talk and talk, on the same subject. This is where I would get off the bus after high school, sit by mom while she was sewing and listen to her talk for a few hours.

Son: Remember earlier, I referenced about being a mediator between the two for a season. This is where dad focused on the responses from mom; when he made the sincere effort to connect with mom at a deeper level.

Son: From sincere trail and error, dad mastered at talking with mom at a deeper level, but not for hours and hours. He would acknowledge and be a part of the deep conversation, but *get to the point much quicker* and have the same effects of a four-to-five-hour conversation. Once he saw mom respond back in a satisfied way, then he would change the subject to …. *Let's go do this.* Mom loved to go do things. So, she became satisfied with both, the some what deeper to the point conversation and going to do something she liked.

Son: After dad having continual success with this, he was convinced it was crucial in any relationship, to have a good relationship.

Son: It took dad almost two decades to master this. Yup. With all the hellish events that took place in dad's life, mom's diabetes handicaps and suicide attempt.

Son: Dad knew if he couldn't make this sincere attempt to connect at a deeper level with mom, she was going to find away out of the relationship. Period. Bus ticket or no bus ticket, GONE.

Son: Once dad's new discovery of connecting with mom in deeper way kicked in; then he went back over the events in his life with mom, and realized their relationship would have been a whole lot more enriching. *Times two.*

Son: Real genuine love for each other relationship; only deserves the best communication in reaching those surreal enriching moments together… *as though they are one spirit, one mind and one body;* thoroughly enjoying their life journey together.

79. When going on dates make sure the other one is having fun and focus on them only.

Son: Dad, was a master of being "ALL IN" on autopilot, especially having fun doing anything anywhere. From building the next home we would be living in, farming, mowing the yard, to sitting around the camp fire.

Son: Again dad, learned this personally, when going through his season of learning how to have deeper conversations with mom. He showed in his actions, versus having a four-to-five-hour conversation. It was brilliant on dad's part. His actions spoke volumes.

Son: When on the dance floor; dad would dance with mom, like they were the only two in the room. Mom could feel it and you could see it on her face.

Son: Mom's mental relationship with dad was healing up sooo much faster with this one on one; the only one dad focused on, when going on a date with mom.

Son: *Why am I talking like I was there?* I was a few times. Dad would take us to someone's else's party and turn it into going on a date with mom.

Son: What's even cooler times ten is ... Mom got so mentally healed up in her deeper but to the point conversation with dad and dad focusing on her, like he was on a date with her. They would get their focus on each date night done in ten minutes, then go through the crowds with each other. Connecting with the crowds in a deep way, to the point the people in the crowds would start laughing out loud. One section after another. Dad and mom as a team would work that whole crowd to the point, they were the life of the party.

Son: It blew my mind, as I personally witnessed this first hand a few times. That party at first was going nowhere fast until mom and dad made their way in the crowd. When comparing the beginning to the end of the same party – it was two different parties. *I swear.*

82. Travel Before Having Kids; if You Like to Travel. Travel First. Get Traveling Done First.

Son: Dad and mom took their traveling seriously and seriously had fun, while traveling.

Son: Nothing's wrong with traveling with children, it's just two different mindsets.

Son: One mindset is just the two of them. They can be "ALL IN" with each other. Enjoying the scenery, the silence and the action moments together; without any distractions. Priceless. *The only time to appreciate this experience is before having children.*

Son: Years later, enjoy traveling with our children. Focusing on the whole family enjoying the scenery, the silence and the action moments together; without distractions.

Son: Now if we didn't do the traveling before, we had children; would be looking at each other thinking how we can leave the children for a few minutes, to squeeze in a few enjoyable moments by ourselves. That thought alone, confirms we should travel before having children.

Son: This also sets the tone, of waiting a few years before having children. Being able to enjoy each other up front versus waiting for all the children to leave home; then for the first time enjoy each other, by yourselves.

Son: Now enjoying each other upfront before having children, will make enjoying each other after all the children leave home, that more enriching. It will be like a pick up, where we left off experience.

Son: Dad and mom waited seven years before having children. They did a lot of traveling together, plus.

Son: Then being a witnessing on the back side; when I left home, dad and mom did just that.

Son: They picked up where they left off. But this time went all in and bought a vacation home, in a warm weather winter state. They enjoyed a lot of winters there and used it to travel to other places. This allowed them to take traveling together at a whole new level, because of their traveling before having children years. They were experienced versus being newbies.

95. Have Two Wills, One for Yourself and One for Your Spouse; the Survivor Might Have Different Plans.

Son: Dad was thoroughly convinced, to the point, he didn't want anything to do with setting up the will/trust. He left that up to mom. Period. He didn't care. **Repeat 2.0** *This Soberly Kicks in Like NO OTHER.*

Son: **Until mom passed on before him.** He realized everything was set up against him, because mom set up as, if she was the last one standing. Mom looked at, *I don't want to be responsible for the up keep on their home and cabin... especially during all those seasonal changes.* So, she sets in motion the plans to sell them both and move in with someone. Dad wanted his home and cabin, *he built with his own hands.* He loved doing DIY projects. Those were Dad's life blood flowing pride and joys. Dad would even joke when mom was here sitting next to him. *"**I would rather divorce my wife then sell the cabin.**"* Then laugh. I was right there, and heard with my own ears.

Son: It defiantly wasn't easy to untangle the mess with and for dad, because mom *had it **all legally** set up* as though she was living here longer than dad.

Son: There was a lot of knots to untie, so that he could THEN untangle the whole yarn ball.

Son: Dad took **a lot** of sobering hits by people, he thought loved him and was looking out for his best interests. Acquaintances, Professionals and the likes. **NOT.** This woke dad up to the point; he didn't want and or associate with them any longer. Doctors, Lawyers, Etc. When dad put them on the spot, they cowardly hide behind their staff. Total 180 in their personalities. It was common to see shame on their faces, but gutless to makes amends for dad.

Son: *Dad would end up soberly laughing* about finding out how people really are, after someone dies. He would mention references to when his dad passed on. How some family members very rarely would visit him and soon as he died, they would be "so concerned" and act like they were the bests of friends forever.

Son: Me helping dad through this process, put a target on my back and personally took some sobering hits too. Watching people come from every direction, *like concerned vultures* hoping to get a quick snack on its vulnerable prey.

Son: *But we got through it, didn't we dad.* The mess was finally cleaned up. All the vultures flew away. None of them to be found anywhere. *What's more sobering* none of them never came back to deepen their friendship with dad. It's like they wrote him off.

Son: **UNTIL Dad passed on... YUP. THEIR BACK** and with unsubstantiated premises, why their entitled to everything. It's amazing how self-centered people act and live.

Son: Dad and I was able to enjoy the last couple of years of dad's life together before transitioning on to be with his free movie sweet heart.

Son: Looking back, dad now realizes it starts with just taking care of the basics handling of money. Buying groceries, paying bills and necessities. 2.0 Then with that experience together; add the estate planning with a two-plan option, to cover all their bases. ***For Each Other's Best Interest.***

97. Don't Spend Much on Weddings. Just enough to get it done. The money is going to last long or short. When get married in younger years don't have a lot of money.

Son: Me witnessing the marriage from my personal perspective, even this long ago and *so glad my ex did leave me.* I agree with dad.

Son: It seems like it's a special event that I want my family and friends to enjoy. But how much time does everyone get to spend with the bride and groom? A few minutes? Every thing is moving so fast, the guests are basically there watching a wedding show in real time.

Son: Then the money and coordinating all the details for the expected crowd size.

Son: It would be more cost effective to have someone record it, put it on a wedding website and take donations or mail them a wedding gift. Then the bride and groom visit them at a later date. The one-on-one experience for 30 to 60 minutes would be more memorable.

Son: Dad saw this and realized afterwards; they would have been better off, just getting married without the expenses of catering to a crowd. They could save the money and or take a better trip together somewhere special too them.

Son: The bride and groom would be able to enjoy their special day even more; versus stopping randomly every few minutes to be respectful, to hear loved ones say... *congratulations... you look beautiful together .... plus, a bunch more nice-things ...*

Son: Plus-plus sending out all those invitations and thank you notes. You know the cost of a postage stamp now a days? Crazy.

Son: If that's to dramatical of a change, then do a hybrid version. Have a private marriage ceremony then meet up for the reception later. But this is still at the cost of the bride and groom.

Son: Unless you have a buy your own reception. Lol. At least you would see how many people really want to come to your reception, if their willing to buy their own meal. The price of the meal would cover catering, hall rental and decorations. BUT... before the bride and groom commit, a minimum-meals purchased have to be committed first. Do not want to get stuck with cost of catering and the hall, when only one family shows up. ☺

Son: Going full circle on dad's point, it's just better not spend all that money. Especially if you don't have it to begin with. If do have the money, then it's worth even more to take a better and or longer honey moon. Making this special moment, even more enriching for the both of you.

Son: *Just an fyi, if I ever get married again, that's exactly what I'm doing. Even if money isn't a problem. It makes perfect sense. Thanks again for the advice pops!*

99. Learn How to Love with Your Actions; Have Fun Loving with Your Actions. Do it until it's automatically Natural so You Can Enjoy Loving with Your Actions.

Son: Dad had to learn this one hard way. Remember what we mentioned earlier, about that tough season mom and dad went through? No matter how much dad tried to talk in a deeper way, mom never bought it.

Son: For several years, it was frustrating to dad; that he wasn't able to connect with mom at a deeper level. After trying everything dad knew, he went old school. He showed her by his actions, he was understanding what she was talking about at a deeper level.

Son: Being an "ALL IN" guy, dad was automatically loving mom with his actions, in no time.

Son: The best part was, they didn't have to waste all that time hoping and trying to get to the point... to prove a point. They both now; knew each other, knew the point and could get back to having fun loving each other.

103. When Your Lover and or Child Passes before You, Keep Them Close to Your Heart so You will Keep Communicating with Them. That Continual Fellowship will be Good Medicine for Your Life.

Son: Dad missed mom like no other when she passed on. His whole life came crashing down. He was convinced with all his hellish events he had in his life; he swore his was passing on before mom. He would comment from time to time, that mom deserves to live longer than him.

Son: As mentioned before, he had pictures of mom in every room and every where in that room.

Son: It was defiantly good medicine to dad. But me personally observing him, it wasn't enough. It's like it reminded him on how much he really missed her.

Son: Me being a book writer of a loving dad, I had to take it a step farther.

Son: I started to ask questions about his life with mom, how he met her and what was it like living life with her. *Dad lit up like a thousand* christmas trees.

Son: When I got his life story published, I bought fifty copies of his book. Took the box of books to him at his house and had him open the box. He was clueless. And acting like it was his birthday.

Son: I had the camera ready to get his first impression in finding out, what was really in the box.

Son: *Priceless*. He had the biggest smile on his face, that I haven't seen in a long time. And then started crying and thanking me, like no other.

Son: Dad was so proud of his life story journey with mom book; he was handing it out to all his favorite people in his life.

Son: Writing and publishing dad's life story with mom; gave him a lot of good medicine, for about a couple of years.

Son: Then having his published book wasn't enough later on. He truly missed actually being physically around mom.

Son: Even though the book effect wore off, I have no regrets writing and publishing it for him. It was priceless times a thousand. Seriously. It brought honorable closure to that season of dad's life with mom. And to mine as well as a son to them. *It was like the best thank you I could give my dad and mom; for all the things they taught me about what it takes to have a more enriching life, in our life journey.*

Son: Even though dad missed mom, he became more at peace with himself.

Son: *I highly encourage everyone* to help write their parents life story while their both living and or at least with the surviving spouse. And have the book published, so they can hold it in their hands.

Son: The look on my dad's face; while touching his book for the first time, *was priceless times ten thousand.*

☥ Family Survival Tips ☥
QTY 15

32. **If You're Young Have More Children.** Makes a healthy family; to me it does. Altogether, some help one another. Older ones will carry the smaller ones on their backs. Bigger families are better.

Son: Dad goes back and forth on this one; larger to smaller to larger. Good points for both options.

Son: Going between spending more time individually with each child, to the children having more siblings to play with.

Son: Having children at a younger age, does wake me up to having to be more responsible, sticking to schedules and teaching little ones a lot of fundamental skills.

Son: If you and your spouse have a two-way relationship then having children at a younger age, will deepen your two-way relationship. Big time.

Son: Having more children does allow the children to learn how to help each other out. I can personally vouch for that. BUT. And this is a **BIG BUT**. Only if the child has a caring heart. Thinks of others, at times more than themselves. If the child is self-centered and or even a soft version of self-centerism, then that child will not help out. *Period.*

Son: Example: A family with three children. It's not a small family nor a large family, but enough for the children to have some siblings. If two of these children are self-centered and or a soft version of being self-centered and the third is compassionate towards others... Then the family as a greater whole will and can have fun with each other, but the individual children will not be connecting in a deep way. *Period.*

Son: The compassionate child will try to connect to the other siblings, but it will only be surface deep. As they get older, they will separate and not connect with each other. But the compassionate child will try and keeping hoping, they will someday.

Son: Summary. A larger family does create a larger experience; but should consider the inner dynamics of how the children, will really connect with their siblings. *The sobering reality will be dealing with self-centered children.* They will continually push boundaries, regardless of how much discipline they get. Knowing this tip upfront, will give us an advantage as a parent. Versus wasting a lot of time learning it along the way.

Son: Extra point on connecting with our children. The first question we need to ask ourselves, up front is... *is this relationship with my child a two-way relationship.* As the child gets older, are they making/wanting to make a deeper connection with me as a parent? If it's just surface, then the odds are high they are self-centered and or a soft version of being self-centered.

Son: A soft version of self-centerism is the child's/person's words sound caring and understanding. BUT their actions are the opposite. As they get older as adults, they very rarely... if not at all ... contact family. If they do, it's short and communication sounds concerning. But ends up with, I got to go. Every time. *Sobering to a good parent.*

Son: Learn how to read children and people actions; versus what they are talking about. This will give us the advantage point; on how to take any hopes of a deeper relationship in baby steps, with our child. And as the child becomes adult and maybe have children themselves.

57. A lot of brothers and sisters means you'll have someone to play with and Keep Out of Mom's and Dad's Hair. They might give you a haircut.

Son: Lol. Dad came from a family of seven children. Dad was a twin to his sister.

Son: The only things I remember dad talking about playing is: hide and seek, wrestling, making ice-cream, squirting cow's milk at each other, going to the free movies and ice skating on the family's farm pond. I'm sure he did a lot more other things, but those are the ones he would keep highlighting.

Son: Of those his favorites were, making ice-cream after most of his family went to town. He stayed back, *cranked it and ate it.* He was always smiling, every time he told the story.

Son: Then another, ice skating with his twin sister on the family's farm pond. At that time, funds were tight and they only had one pair of skates. So, his sister put on one skate and dad put on the other skate. They would hold each other, with their arms on each other's backs. Then proceed to skate on the pond like they were one person. Dad thought that was so cool bonding with his sister that way.

Son: This was back in the day when there were no electronic games, cell phones, etc. They didn't have any board games either. It was having fun with what they didn't have. *Yup.* So, it was a lot easier to get outside and playing with whatever they had or didn't have,

Son: Having bigger families meant having more options in keeping busy with someone. Especially if mom and dad couldn't play at the time.

Son: It was more of dad getting his rearend whipped by his dad *often*, then getting a haircut. *Lol.* Enough so, that dad would go down the road a couple of miles to his friends place and they go of and get into trouble together.

63. Before You Get a Pet for Your Child be Willing to Take Care of it Yourself. If not, it would be better to spend that time with your child. You're with them the shortest amount of time.

Son: Really wouldn't have to add any more to that. It speaks for itself.

Son: Dad ended up getting us a dog, his nick name was Smug. Dad and mom surprised us on one of our coming back, from an out of state trip to see mom's mother. I took a liking to smug the first and second time I saw him. We had two dogs to choose from. Smug would naturally wanting to hang out with me, then everyone else.

Son: I naturally loved animals, so feeding and taking care of Smug was easy. He would go around with me; checking up on all the other animals and feeding them, taking care of them. *AAAAANNND....* Then play with all of them. Me and Smug; had a blast being best friends, and with the rest of the animals on dad's farm.

Son: And every night; at bed time without asking, Smug would jump onto my bed, snuggled up to me and we would fall to sleep together. *Priceless.* Thank you, Dad millions.

Son: And agreed with dad, if I didn't naturally take care of Smug, dad would have been.

64. Play with Your Grand Children.

Son: Priceless.

Son: It's easier when you love embracing being a parent; and harnessing naturally wanting a deeper enriching relationship, with your children.

Son: Now as a grandparent it makes the experience more enriching; interacting with your children's children.

Son: It also creates a deeper bond with your child, when your child sees you interacting with their child. It helps solidifies your relationship with your child.

Son: Your grand child gets a taste of what their parent experience; when they were playing with you, as a child.

Son: Play with a sincere "All In" heart. The child can sense if you really want to play with them or not.

66. Family Vacations are the Best. It seems like it is.

Son: Dad was an "All In" guy and dad. So, it would be the icing on the cake, from all those other great-play have fun moments, dad had with us.

Son: Going on vacation with dad and mom was also like a pat on the back, for being a good and extremely helpful son.

Son: Plus, it exposed me to a bigger land mass, with different cities and cultures; while in the comfort of dad and mom, by my side.

Son: What made the vacations even more special, was each one of them, had a unique special memory attached to it.

74. Have at Least One Boy and One Girl Before Stop Having Children, so that They can Relate to Each Other.

Son: I can vouch for that.

Son: Dad picked up on this, after the fact he only had two boys.

Son: Growing up, I noticed dad interacting with women was easy.

Son: I had no clue. Yah, I had a mother, but she was my mom. I had no choice to inner act with her in any other way. If I did, she wouldn't be my mom then.

Son: Not having a sister, it was at first awkward and or strange talking to a girl to me.

Son: I as a father; wanted to have at least one boy and one girl, to have that complete experience of being a parent. *Obviously* the two genders have different needs.

Son: After having two girls and one boy, some what helped me out with interacting with girls/women.

Son: Some of you might be saying, *wait you had a wife ... wasn't you interacting with her?*

Son: I thought I was, but looking back it was a one-way relationship. I was always the one giving into the relationship, she never gave back in a deeper way. **NEVER.**

Son: Way long after my children moved on and had families of their own. I made up my mind ... it's time to learn how to have a deeper communication, two-way relationship with a woman.

Son: One of my daughters was a very caring put family always first, daughters. Since my communication skills was from the man's perspective, I was always head butting with my daughter. If I was going to ever master this, then it would have to be with her first.

Son: It took me several months, to understand how women think, their priorities and their challenges. Once enough of it sunk it; I would test my new communication skills, with my daughter in baby steps.

Son: What made the challenge even harder was, every one – even women – take my daughter wrong. So, I thought; if I can really and honestly connect a deeper two conversation communication with my daughter, then I can with any girl or woman.

Son: Even though I fell down; trying to take some baby steps in mastering how to have a two-way conversation relationship with my daughter, I kept at it. At the right sensitive moments versus push-push, like I was trying to win a race.

Son: Then slowly one break through after another over a few months, I was on my way to mastering how to communicate with women.

Son: Today, me and my daughter have super deep two-way conversations. And are closer than ever before.

Son: To master this more, I would have sincere conversations with women in public, at the appropriate times.

Son: *Thank you, dad…for emphasizing the importance of having at least one boy and one girl* before stop having children. Priceless.

Son: *Thank you, daughter…*for giving me the chance to harness mastering having two-way conversations with women. **Priceless 100.0**

75. The More Children You Have the Easier it is to Raise Them. The Oldest Helps Out.

Son: Dad, having experience from both sizes of family's; his family of nine growing up in and having two children himself family. Made it clear to him, the oldest does help out.

Son: Me personally, watching my own and my children having children first hand. This was priceless watching the older sibling sincerely wanting to help the baby sister or brother out. In their own child like way. No matter how helpless they were, they still wanted to help out.

Son: It's precious and priceless at the same time. Nothing even comes close to a toddler sincerely trying to help out their baby sister or brother.

Son: Especially in a healthy good family setting with mom and dad, lovingly observing it together

80. Babies give us a sense of responsibility. I wanted to do it coming from a big family.

Son: Real Hard Real Fast. Especially if you weren't planning on it. It's priceless to see the other parents face, when they hear…. *hey honey. WE ARE going to have a baby.* 😊

Son: In my dad's case. Yup. He was "All In" having family.

Son: Mom found out she was pregnant with me; on one of their long southern states traveling trip, they loved taking.

Son: Looking back now, I'm thinking it was mom that was the one who only wanted two children. Because dad has talked more about having bigger families then smaller ones.

Son: And when I'm really honest with myself – even though mom taught me some really good life skills – she never wanted to have a deeper two-way conversation with me. It was always me listening to her.

Son: Even when the kids were laughing at me with my 3rd grade butch haircut. After I explained it all, all she said was… *did you laugh back?* Helpful advice, but not a deep two-way conversation.

Son: Having less children is less responsibility and the quicker they'll leave home. *Wow.* This is sobering to me now. Absorbing this more, I'm convinced even more now, mom didn't want to have family and or at least have a big family. She didn't want the responsibility.

Son: When we got bigger, she had no problem dropping us off to our cousins, while she was out running the roads with sisters. This gave us the sense of a bigger family, without the responsibilities of having a bigger family. We had a blast playing with our cousins for hours. We were all creative and doing something *new all the time.*

Son: WOW. Revisiting my childhood; while writing this, has been a big eye opener for me. *Thank You **AGAIN** Dad! Seriously 100.0*

Son: Having a baby will make you run towards responsibility or make you run away from it. Period.

81. Wait to Have Kids After Been Married a Few Years.

Son: This is dad's emphasis on traveling with your spouse before having children. If at all, it's imperative that the newlyweds have a few years of time together. It will be good medicine in the long run.

Son: A sets it up for taking being together as a couple to the next level – easier – when all the children leave home.

Son: This allows the couple to get to know each other in a deeper way. Even if they were living together for a tad and decided to make it official by getting married.

Son: The being Official Married Couple; has the couple making an open legal commitment to each, versus the appearance of being a casual relationship. This sends the message to their partner, I'm "ALL IN" with my relationship with you. No matter what we face together, *I'm not leaving you.* Even if the other partner is going through the "motions."

83. When the wife tells you to whip the child, think it's a good idea.

Son: *Lol x 1000.*

Son: Did I tell you dad was an "All In" guy, husband and dad? *Lol.*

Son: Oh, the memories of testing mom. Let me make a few confessions. Maybe I was the reason mom didn't want to have anymore children? 😊

Son: Ok let confession time begin. *No clocks please.*

Son: When I did something; mom didn't like me doing, she would out of the blue smack me on the backside of my head. Without warning.

Son: I started to believe my mom was a **Tibetan Monk of Smack**. Lol.

Son: See wasn't even looking at me. It must have been my words I was saying. The smack would sting enough to get me to stop. Then she would turn around with that signature look; she kept just for this moment to say, *when your dad gets home, he's going to whoop your rearend.* Then put a slight sober smile on her face.

Son: That routine started to condition me to be more selective on my timing; with getting even.

Son: Knowing dad's "All In" heart/mind set, I wasn't going to be able to explain my way out of why I was getting even.

Son: Dad comes through the door. Mom looks at dad with her signature look associated with whip his rearend. Wouldn't ask dad about how his day went. Didn't even say hi. No stalled *rearend whipping luck in mom and dad* discussing anything.

Son: Mom's only words to dad was WHIP HIS REAREND.

Son: Dad walked over to me, like he was going to give me a hug. Lift me up with one hand in the air. My feet were air borne. Lol. Took his belt off with the other hand. *Oooo... the suspense...*

Son: I started twitching big time. In hopes I could do a tuck in roll. No luck. Dad took my twitching and turned into a *merry-go-round whipping pinata ride*. Lol. Yup. I'm laughing about it. Because it doesn't sound like it really happened, BUT IT *REALLY* DID.

Son: If only my rearend could talk, it would vouch for me.

Son: Like I mentioned earlier; after riding on the *merry-go-round whipping pinata ride* a few times, I realized dad was "All In" whipping me every time.

Son: No words, in ended with just being looks he got from mom. It evolved to actions without words. Actions Neck of the Woods. Lol.

Son: *So, to end this set me up...* juice mom to have dad whip me gig, by the person who was egging me on. *We came up with a new strategy*; to let that person get a chance, at riding the *merry-go-round whipping pinata ride*. And seeing their faces from the audience view was priceless. My life got less dramatical at the same time. *Hmm.*

Son: *Thank you, dad*; for teaching me how to talk to people, without saying a word. Lol. *Priceless.*

84. Work Hard to Making the Family Bond Stronger.

Son: Dad, got a slow start on this one. By the time he went through a few hellish events; learning to have deeper two-way conversations with mom and living on the other side of those, he realized he needed to be "All In" with making his family bond stronger.

Son: This ended up being dad's core to and with his "All In" heart/mind set, in everything and anything he did.

Son: Dad's dedication to this; really was the medicine that gave new life to mom and their relationship, as a couple.

Son: To the point; mom and dad was the life of the gathering/party, everywhere they went. I would personally witness this. It was impressive to see everyone loving to be around my mom and dad as a couple. **EVERYWHERE**.

Son: This was refreshing to mom, to being the center of attention in a good way. *She came alive!*

Son: What do they say... *happy wife happy life*. I think dad started that? 😊

Son: One last strong point. Remember this can't be forced. It can't be fake. It's **gottsa** be all natural, automatically compassionately coming from the heart and mindset in everything anywhere. And we respectively learn it in baby steps.

Son: ALL These Tips will put that process for you on steroids. Cut your time to learn at least in half, if not quicker.

Son: **PLUS**. Remember. R*emember* and *Remember.* Less is More and Slow is Faster.

85. Never too Old to be a Grand Parent. To be a grandparent you re are going to be a little older. They look like grandparents. If you look like a grandparent might as well be one.

Son: Lol. Dad's wit and humor is at it again. *Deep.*

Son: Dad's "All In" heart/mind set; was again the core for him to having fun with people, children and grandchildren. He was always hospitable. Dad knew how to remove the tension, between people.

Son: Dad learned this one later in life. Knowing now his determination in having a deeper two-way conversation with mom, was detrimental to their relationship moving forward.

Son: If there isn't going to be any hopes of a two-way relationship with their child, then more than likely they won't be one with their grandchild – due to their child. Maybe when the grandchild gets older and out on their own.

Son: Regardless of the relationship statuses, always be open to sincerely be that grandparent *they need anytime anywhere.* They look up to us, because of our ages. It's naturally subconscious thinking. *Their older than me, they must know a lot, what are their life stories? ...*

91. Thank Your Loved Ones for Hanging in There and around; if They Didn't we wouldn't be Where We are Today.

Son: True. *But sobering.*

Son: Dad has a lot of stories, to prove that tip over and over again. From all those near-death hellish events in his life: the family pet ram, Korea, vehicle accidents, heart attack, multiple bypasses, being shoved into a nursing home and then almost straight jacket confinement. If there wasn't a caring individual in dad's life at those times, then he would have been long gone. Period.

Son: Dad recognizes this and *he showed his sincere* appreciation for what they did for him, in many different ways.

100. The Best Advice a Father can Tell His Son is "Hang onto Your Money."

Son: *Dad…*

Son: If only we could learn this lesson up front versus rationalizing in my heart/mind set that, I'm different and it's ok do, this time.

Son: Dad learned this one later in his life too. With Dad's "All In" heart/mind set; he was always in a … it will work out mode.

Son: As he retired; had fun with mom in retirement traveling different locations, mom's family passing on and finding themselves with more alone time versus go… go … go. It became more obvious to dad, that they should have toned it down a tad.

Son: Personally, I was fortunate to just start out without this advice, to just do cash. If didn't have the cash then I didn't do it… then the my divorce slapped me out of that reality.

Son: Making ends meet was tough. Made tough sacrifices to build that foundation back up again. Once I got my children back, then I went back to doing just cash.

Son: That worked a tad until I realized my children are growing up fast and I wanted them to experience a real home life *versus living at an apartment.* Nothing against apartments. I just rationalized that it will hurt like hell; but let's get the home, have the fun and I'll pay for it when they all move out on their own. Blew the cement right out of my foundation of cash only decisions.

Son: Dug myself out, repaired the damage and back at it again. Then life happens and I would justify myself of doing the wash and dry repeat cycles.

Son: And now find myself again digging myself out of my justified messes.

Son: *I said all that to say this.* The way everything turned out, I would have been better off sticking to doing cash only decisions. I would have had to make a lot more sacrifices but odds are high, I would have had *somewhat* the same outcomes – if not better.

Son: I can say this now, learning from cash only to living on credit cards. *We are not taught enough, about having multiple income streams.* Versus going all in on one job source income. We get locked in and try to milk it as much as we can. And nothing but.

Son: But in reality, we should be thinking about having more income streams versus automatically throwing it on a credit card – pay it later. Up front versus being shoved in a corner and having to make a decision now. But can't.

Son: *A step farther with this.* I got my main source of income routine down to where I can do it automatically naturally. Now focus on my spare time; in creating another income routine. Once mastered another one. Now we're up to three income streams. Now if we want to update our used car to a newer updated used car, we can with the new income stream, without affecting the first income stream.

Son: The goal is … I only make decisions based on if I have enough income coming in; plus have another income stream on the back side, to cover random emergency bills.

Son: This heart/mindset increases my odds on holding my money longer and lowers my risks with random emergencies. Even worse case, I lose my job to "downsizing"? .... No problem. I have another source of income to cover immediate needs. *Now I have another 30 to 50 hours of free time to work on another new income stream.*

Son: They don't teach us this stuff. Period. Let alone our parents showing us by example.

Son: Dad and I had to learn this the sobering hard way to get to the point of being "All In" with this tip.

Son: *You get this tip for just the cost of this book...* hopefully it's not too late for ourselves and our loved ones; to harnessing this naturally and automatically extra tip.

101. The Best Advice a Father can Tell His Daughter is "Stay Away from Drunks; They'll Ruin Your Life."

Son: ***Wow dad.*** We finally made it to your last tip.

Son: This is ironic for dad to say. Dad never had a daughter, to be able to say it to her.

Son: This one came on dad's personal experience over time.

Son: Dad's dad was a drunk, but he could hold his alcohol. No matter what kind of bar fight he was in, he whopped their rearends big time. They all ended up respecting him all the more and stopped fighting him.

Son: Note: You might to want research this yourself. I've heard of people who have the bacteria in their digestive systems, that feed off alcohol and break it down fast. To the point, it doesn't affect the person.

Son: Dad knew a few couples close in his life; that were the bad beat your rearend drunks, to their wives. Back in the day, divorce wasn't legal. If you married a drunk then you were stuck with them the rest of your life. Disheartening. BUT...

Son: BUT... if I was honest with myself upfront then I would have never married that individual in the first place. BASED ON THEIR ACTIONS... Actions speak louder than the person's word. Every time and Anywhere. Period.

Son: I do believe though, with all of dad's experiences he had with drunks, by the time he started having children with mom. He would have told his daughter not to marry a drunk.

Son:

And with that, we'll let dad have the last word. *Since these are all of dad's Hell and Back Survival Tips; to help us navigate through our lives and hopefully avoid the hellish events, that try to randomly occur in our lives.*

Son: *Here's to US Having MORE Enriching Relationships and Lives Everyone!* ***times a thousand!!***

‡ Tribute to an Awesome Dad ‡

Son: This felt like to me what people say, this is an Opportunity of a Lifetime. Being able to hang out with Dad, in his own home and time and write down the wisdom he learned from his accumulated life experiences. He grew up on a farm that supported the community. Fell in love with his thirteen-year-old sweet heart and never left her side in the good times and bad times. He went to the eighth grade. Raised gladiolas from the rich farm creek banks then sold a dozen of them for seventy-five cents to guys getting out of work. Starting from Dirt and Successful Flower shop owner that employed twelve people. Drafted into the Korean War; Married, waited seven years to have kids. Had two children, has seven great grandchildren, married 62 yrs. He knows how to build a home from the ground up inside and out, built four homes, and remodeled a farm house, built two cabins after working 40 hr. weeks at his career job. On the edges of death: vehicle accident, heart attack and bypass surgery. He cared for his diabetic wife for forty plus years. Travel out west three times and to southern warm state over 20 plus times. Where he bought a trailer home and lived there in the winter months for several years. He went on cruises. He was the secretary of Local Veterans Hall. He helped people build their cabins, repair their vehicles, volunteer for several non-profits. He learned how to fly a single engine air plane. He was a widow for a little more than four years. He did all this without rushing. It came natural to him to stay busy. He would never let you know he was in a rush, in pain and or having a bad day. I never saw dad having a bad day, where it pissed him off and it affected everyone around him. He was never angry at people and life. He was and is a master at going with the flow and being at peace with it. He wasn't rich to do all these things; he had to rejuggle his resources to make it happen. He's just a normal man, who blends in at any local grocery and department store. He was never into the bling bling movement; wearing clothes and accessories to get attention.

Son: He stood out in connecting with his loved ones around him, in everyday life while at the same time compassionately fitting in with the crowds as a common man. He listens more than he talks. His actions are honorable, ethical and gentle. He only expresses his love in and with his actions. He is wise, humorous and driven. He worked hard, played hard and slept hard while being at peace with his environment; automatically, naturally to the point he enjoys it.

Son: Writing dad's life story for him is and was priceless. It was a way of repaying dad back; for all what he has done for me, throughout my life. I got to learn more about myself and how to be at peace with oneself.

Son: Every child should set down with their parents and ask them million+ questions about their lives and publish it in book form. The mindset of publishing my parent's life story; will cause me to thoroughly ask questions about my parents' life changing events versus random brief conversations about their life. This format of listening, writing and rereading their life story; will create a stronger bond between the child and the parent. This stronger bond will bring closure to the child and parents past, present and future relationship with each other. This closure will allow the child and the parent to grow their current relationship into a more enriching relationship.

Son: Dad did you ever think you would have a son who would ask you all these questions?

Dad: No.

Son: Didn't see it coming?

Dad: No. (*Dad Chuckles*).

Son: *Thank you, Dad!* A lot of these Hell and Back Survival Tips made me; smile, think and want to try, especially if I get the opportunity to marry and have a family. Lol

✝ Index ✝

Printed in the USA
CPSIA information can be obtained
at www.ICGtesting.com
CBHW071845140424
6855CB00008B/82